UN Peace-keeping Operations: A Guide to Japanese Policies

UN PEACE-KEEPING OPERATIONS: A GUIDE TO JAPANESE POLICIES

By L. William Heinrich Jr., Akiho Shibata, and Yoshihide Soeya

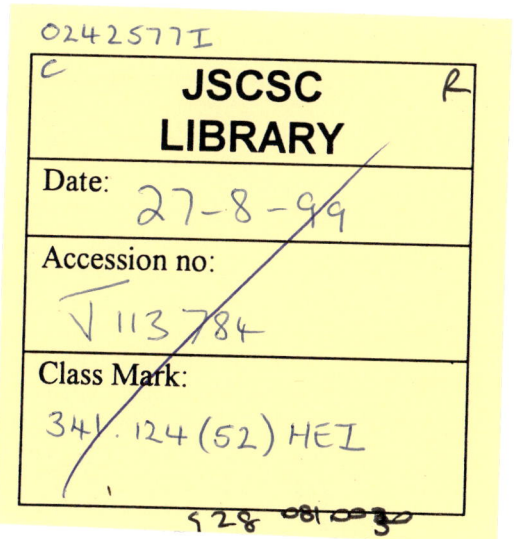

United Nations University Press

TOKYO · NEW YORK · PARIS

United Nations University Press
The United Nations University, 53-70, Jingumae 5-chome,
Shibuya-ku, Tokyo 150-8925, Japan
Tel: +81-3-3499-2811   Fax: +81-3-3406-7345
E-mail: sales@hq.unu.edu
http://www.unu.edu

United Nations University Office in North America
2 United Nations Plaza, Room DC2-1462-70, New York, NY 10017, USA
Tel: +1-212-963-6387   Fax: +1-212-371-9454
E-mail: unuona@igc.apc.org

United Nations University Press is the publishing division of the United Nations University.

Cover design by Joyce C. Weston
Cover photo by Takashi Kakinuma/Nippon Koho Center

Printed in the United States of America

UNUP-1003
ISBN 92-808-1003-0

Library of Congress Cataloging-in-Publication Data
Heinrich, L. William (Lawrence William), 1958–
UN peace-keeing operation : a guide to Japanese policies / by L. William
Heinrich Jr., Akiho Shibata, and Yoshihide Soeya.
    p. cm.
Includes bibliographical references and index.
ISBN 9280810030 (pbk.)
1. United Nations-Armed Forces. 2. United Nations-Japan. 3.
Japan-Armed Forces-Foreign countries. 4. Military law-Japan. I.
Shibata, Akiho, 1965–   II. Soeya, Yoshihide, 1955–   III. Title. IV.
Title: United Nations peace-keeping operations
JZ6377.J3 H45   1999
355.3′57–dc21   99-6052
                                                            CIP

CONTENTS

ACRONYMS

AMDA	Association of Medical Doctors in Asia
ASDF	Air Self-Defence Forces
CIVPOL	Civilian Police
DSP	Democratic Socialist Party
GSDF	Ground Self-Defence Forces
IPCA	International Peace Cooperation Assignment
IPCHQ	International Peace Cooperation Headquarters
JSP	Japan Socialist Party
LDP	Liberal Democratic Party
MOFA	Ministry of Foreign Affairs
MOVECON	Movement Control
MSDF	Maritime Self-Defence Forces
ONUC	UN Operation in the Congo
ONUMOZ	UN Operation in Mozambique
ONUSAL	UN Observer Mission in El Salvador
ONUVEN	UN Observation Mission for Elections in Nicaragua
PKF	peace-keeping force
PKO	peace-keeping operation
SDF	Self-Defence Forces

SDPJ	Social Democratic Party of Japan (formerly the JSP)
UAR	United Arab Republic
UNAVEM	UN Angola Verification Mission
UNDOF	UN Disengagement Observer Force (Golan Heights)
UNFICYP	UN (Peace-keeping) Force in Cyprus
UNGOMAP	UN Good Offices Mission in Afghanistan and Pakistan
UNHCR	UN High Commissioner for Refugees
UNIIMOG	UN Iran–Iraq Military Observer Group
UNIKOM	UN Iraq–Kuwait Observation Mission
UNITAF	Unified Task Force (Somalia)
UNOGIL	UN Observation Group in Lebanon
UNOSOM	UN Operation in Somalia
UNPROFOR	UN Protection Force (former Yugoslavia)
UNSAS	UN Stand-by Arrangements System
UNTAC	UN Transitional Authority in Cambodia
UNTAG	UN Transition Assistance Group (Namibia)
UNTSO	UN Truce Supervision Organization

INTRODUCTION

Japan's policy on UN peace operations

This handbook covers the main aspects of Japan's policy on UN peace operations. The term "peace operation" refers to both civilian and military efforts under the direction of the United Nations for the purpose of preventing, terminating, or recovering from conflicts. This volume aims to provide the reader with a better understanding of the political, legal, and economic factors that shape Japan's policy toward both military and civilian participation in these operations.

The issue of whether and how Japan should participate in collective security – a broad term that encompasses UN peace operations – has been the subject of profound disagreement in Japan from the moment the United Nations came into existence in 1945. In the years following the 1954 decision to re-establish a full-fledged military organization (the Self-Defence Forces – SDF), a fundamental tension developed between conservative political forces, which claimed that Japan had a responsibility to cooperate with the United Nations for global peace and security, and progressive political forces, which urged restraint in using military force. Despite the concerted efforts of the Ministry of Foreign Affairs, opponents of the military effectively barred the SDF from participating in UN peace operations throughout the Cold War period, an outcome that was strongly supported by a number of East Asian countries. The periodic policy debates that arose in this period are dealt with at some length in chapter 1.

Japan's recent experiences in UN peace operations are covered in chapter 2, while aspects of the decision-making process are highlighted in chapter 3. In the past five years, the Japanese government has sent the SDF to three peace-keeping missions and one humanitarian relief operation, but has rejected numerous other requests for assistance. Each time the Japanese government proposes an operation, the governing parties must examine every aspect of the plan to ensure that the conditions imposed by Japanese laws have been met and that the risks to Japanese personnel are acceptably low. Changes in the domestic political system unleashed by the end of one-party rule in 1993 have yet to alter the government's cautious approach significantly, and tensions between progressives and conservatives continue to impede the decision-making process.

The legal aspects of Japanese policy are dealt with expertly and authoritatively in chapter 4. The focus is the Peace-keeping Law, which was passed after more than a year of arduous negotiations and debate in parliament (the national Diet). By permitting the SDF to take part in less risky peace operations, the law opened the way for Japan to embark on a new phase in its UN policy. Whereas in the eyes of many foreign observers the law was merely a modest revision to existing policy, to the Japanese it was an important step forward after years of political stalemate.

Financial and budgetary aspects of Japanese policy are briefly covered in chapter 5. Despite the sharp downturn in Japanese economic growth during the 1990s, fiscal constraints have not had a significant impact on Japanese participation in UN peace operations. Although it is true that the SDF has been sent to only four operations, this is due to the government's cautious approach to dispatching the SDF abroad, rather than to any fiscal barriers. As a percentage of the total defence budget, peace-keeping expenditures are quite small, suggesting that the Japanese government could afford to take part in other operations.

The third part of the handbook covers Japanese military and civilian participation in UN peace operations. Chapter 6 discusses the SDF role in each of the UN peace operations in which Japan has participated: Cambodia (UNTAC), Mozambique (ONUMOZ), Zaire (a humanitarian operation to aid Rwandan refugees), and the Golan Heights (UNDOF). Chapter 7 highlights the civilian component of Japan's participation in UN peace operations, an aspect that has received far less attention than military participation. (In this case "civilian" refers to non-military sectors, including both government and private institutions that cooperate with the United Nations.) Only in the past few years have Japanese non-governmental organizations (NGOs) begun to make an impact on UN and other international relief efforts, and their influence is likely to grow as the government finds itself unable to manage all aspects of Japan's international relations.

About the authors

Professor *Akiho Shibata* is professor of law at Okayama University in Okayama, Japan, and an expert on the legal aspects of Japan's peace-keeping policy; Professor *Yoshihide Soeya* is professor of political science at Keio University in Tokyo, specializing in Japanese foreign policy issues; Dr. *L. William Heinrich Jr.* has recently completed his Ph.D. at Columbia University on the political aspects of Japan's military policy. He now works for the Export Import Bank of Japan in New York City.

PART I

1

HISTORICAL BACKGROUND

Japan's participation in UN peace operations has long suffered from an underlying tension between the country's general support for the United Nations and its deep-seated reluctance to use military force. When the UN General Assembly finally voted to accept Japan's membership in December 1956, it was a proud and symbolic moment, signalling that Japan had taken a major step toward overcoming its badly tarnished reputation. The Ministry of Foreign Affairs (MOFA), with strong public approval, made every effort to play an active role in all facets of the organization because it wished to convince other nations of Japan's desire to be a constructive force in world affairs. But did this include sending armed forces to UN collective security actions?

The devastation of war had created an abiding suspicion among the Japanese toward military organizations and military solutions. This suspicion was manifest in the strong public support for Article 9 of the 1947 constitution, which renounced war and the means to prosecute war, a view that also reassured East Asian countries that had experienced Japanese depredations. Although the Japanese government eventually re-established a military force (the Self-Defence Forces, or SDF), strict limits were placed on how and where it could be deployed. Sending the SDF abroad for any reason was ruled out. Progressive political forces, particularly the Japan Socialist Party and the Japan Communist

Party, strongly favoured this pacifist approach to foreign policy and were intensely critical of government proposals to modify these restrictions. The Liberal Democratic Party (LDP) and other conservative forces were generally willing to acquiesce because they were more concerned with rebuilding the economy.

MOFA, which hoped to play a role in collective security, argued that restrictions on the SDF should not prohibit sending unarmed SDF officers to be part of military observer groups or to perform other non-combat duties, a position that conservative political leaders supported. But the public remained suspicious of the government's intentions in dispatching the SDF abroad, in part because progressive political leaders argued that any loosening of restrictions would lead inexorably to remilitarization. In the specific case of UN military actions, they believed that Japan should refrain from active participation until a true collective security system had been established, rather than a system dominated by the five permanent members. Despite numerous efforts to refute these views, MOFA was unable to win widespread acceptance for SDF participation in the UN peace operations until the 1990s.

Early attempts to join UN peace-keeping operations

On at least two occasions in the 1950s and 1960s, the United Nations requested Japan to send military personnel to peace-keeping operations, perhaps assuming that its self-proclaimed UN-centred diplomacy meant that it would take an active role in collective security. Although MOFA wanted to take part, and believed that the constitution did not in any way bar SDF participation, Japan's conservative political leaders had other important concerns. The main goal was to regain economic prosperity and not to become embroiled in foreign policy issues that diverted the country from this goal. Progressive politicians were only too willing to pounce on any evidence that the conservatives intended to remilitarize Japan in order to create public controversy. As a result, UN requests for Japanese military personnel were rejected despite MOFA support.

The first instance came in 1958, just after Japan had been elected a non-permanent member of the UN Security Council. An internal dispute had arisen in Lebanon over constitutional revision and protest was most vehement among the Muslim sections of the country, especially those areas close to the border with Syria, which was then united with Egypt in the short-lived United Arab Republic (UAR). The Lebanese government, suspecting that the UAR was supporting the unrest, asked the United Nations to consider the matter. On 11 June, the UN Security Council passed a resolution that called for the formation of an observation group (known as the United Nations Observation Group in Lebanon, or UNOGIL) to be dispatched to Lebanon to monitor illegal infiltration of personnel or arms across the Lebanese border. The following day, five officers of what would eventually be a 130-man observation group arrived in Beirut.

Two developments then complicated the situation in Lebanon. The first was the fall of the Hashemite Kingdom in Iraq on 14 July and the installation of a new regime. Lebanon, fearing that unrest in Iraq might spread, asked the United States to send troops to protect its border. The second was a complaint by the Kingdom of Jordan that it, too, suspected the UAR of fomenting domestic unrest. Jordan requested military assistance from Great Britain, which also sent troops. The deployment of British and US troops in the Middle East was strongly opposed by the Soviet Union, and many feared a superpower confrontation in the region. MOFA, taking an unusually independent position, criticized the US action because it undermined Japan's desire to see the United Nations play the primary role in resolving the conflict.

Japan then sought to defuse the situation by proposing on 21 July that the United Nations be permitted to take measures "with a view to enabling the United Nations to fulfill the general purposes established in that resolution [forming UNOGIL], and which will, in accordance with the Charter, serve to ensure the territorial integrity and political independence of Lebanon so as to make possible a withdrawal of the United States forces from Lebanon."[1] One way for the United Nations to carry out its aims in Lebanon was to increase the size of UNOGIL, which numbered only 130 personnel. Although this resolution was ultimately rejected owing to a Soviet veto, Japanese involvement in the Lebanon issue sparked debate in Japan concerning the SDF role in peace-keeping. The creation of UNOGIL had already led the Defence Agency to begin studying whether the SDF might join the operation. Director-General Sato was thought to be enthusiastic about the plan. On 18 July, the head of the Defence Agency's Secretariat indicated that, if asked by the Prime Minister, he would be willing to discuss SDF participation. But an agency study on the matter had already come to the conclusion that, although there were no constitutional obstacles to sending the SDF abroad, it would be advisable to add UN duties to Article 3 of the SDF Law before doing so.

The debate intensified on 28 July when UN Secretary-General Dag Hammarskjöld, believing that the resolution indicated the Japanese government's resolve to participate in UNOGIL, requested that Japan send 10 SDF officers to Lebanon to assist in monitoring the flow of weapons.[2] In the Diet, Foreign Minister Aiichiro Fujiyama, replying to opposition questions, stated that the government was not considering dispatch of the SDF and would not do so, though he did raise the possibility of sending Japanese civilians. The following day, the government decided to reject the UN request. The reason given was that the SDF missions outlined in Article 3 did not include UN duties.

It is certainly true that the SDF Law did not specifically include provisions for sending the SDF abroad, but neither did it forbid such a decision. The Upper House ban on dispatching the SDF abroad was more forthright in prohibiting the dispatch of troops, but, even so, the government could have seconded the officers to MOFA before sending them to Lebanon, thereby avoiding constitutional and legal issues. Instead it chose to reject the UN request, despite its avowed interest in collective security. Behind this decision lay the substantial weight of domestic political opposition to sending the SDF abroad. Neither the progressive parties nor the public were yet prepared to support SDF participation in UN operations. Moderate LDP members, their effort focused on rebuilding the economy, had no intention of supporting MOFA on an issue that had already proved divisive.[3]

The decision not to send the SDF officers to Lebanon received a mixed reaction in the Japanese press. The *Yomiuri* felt that the decision was an acute embarrassment for MOFA because the ministry failed to back its proposal to strengthen the observer group by sending SDF personnel. If the ministry continued to pay lip-service to UN diplomacy, it would seriously impair Japan's international reputation.[4] The *Asahi*, on the other hand, welcomed the decision, arguing that the United Nations should not ask Japan, nor should the Japanese government agree, to send the SDF abroad for any reason.[5] Meanwhile, the United Nations had suffered public rejection by a member country. In subsequent cases the United Nations and Japan pursued a less public approach on security issues. The Japanese government was careful to consider any UN requests through an informal negotiation process. In this way, UN officials could determine whether Japan was predisposed to participate in a particular operation before making a formal public request.

A second instance came on the heels of widespread and intense public dissatisfaction with the Japanese government, which peaked with Prime Minister

Kishi's decision to push ratification of the USA–Japan Security Treaty revisions through the Diet in May 1960. The national mood made the government even more sensitive to public opinion on defence and security issues. When Hayato Ikeda became Prime Minister in July of that year, he deliberately chose to emphasize domestic issues that would appeal to a broad spectrum of the public. In foreign policy, Ikeda adopted a low profile and took few initiatives. One area he felt he could highlight was UN centrism. In one of his first speeches in the Diet, Ikeda declared his intention to increase government support for the United Nations. But a crisis in Africa once again brought the issue of Japanese participation in peace-keeping to public attention.

The newly independent Congo had requested UN troops in July 1960 after Belgium had unilaterally sent forces to restore order in its former colony. The situation was complicated by the subsequent decision by Katanga Province to declare its independence from the Congolese government. During the four-year effort to restore order, the United Nations stationed 20,000 men and women in the Congo, making it the largest peace-keeping operation the United Nations had undertaken to that time.[6] In early 1961, the situation had grown tense following the dismissal and arrest of Prime Minister Patrice Lumumba.

Although there was no formal request for Japanese participation in the operation, there were rumours in Japan that the United Nations had made preliminary enquiries about whether or not Japan would be willing to send troops.[7] Although Hammarskjöld preferred Africans as the main body of the peace-keeping force, Japanese personnel might well have been more welcome than contingents from European countries with colonial ties to the region. Unlike the situation in Lebanon three years earlier, however, the UN personnel were not merely military observers but increasingly involved in trying to quell disturbances. Given the rising tensions in late 1960, the UN Security Council was on the verge of expanding the mandate of the UN Operation in the Congo (ONUC). On 21 February, Resolution 161 was adopted urging ONUC to take all appropriate measures, including the use of force in the last resort, to prevent the occurrence of civil war in the Congo. SDF participation would not be possible in such circumstances.

What ignited public debate in Japan, however, were comments by UN Ambassador Koto Matsudaira, who returned to Japan in early February to give his views on international issues at the Foreign Affairs Deliberation Council

(*Gaiko Mondai Kondankai*). The Council, which Ikeda had formed the previous July, was meant to provide a bridge between the government and the informed public in the aftermath of the unrest that accompanied the revision of the Security Treaty. In remarks made on 21 February, Matsudaira went directly to the core of the dilemma facing Japan's UN diplomats. He began by observing that many believed that Japan should take more positive action in the United Nations to cooperate with the Afro-Asian members. Many of these nations had sent military forces to the UN peace-keeping operation in the Congo, but Japan was prohibited from such assistance. How could Japan claim to pursue UN-centred diplomacy and yet not contribute to peace-keeping operations? He argued that "because the United Nations will be responsible for the future world order, a UN police force ought to be considered. It would not be reasonable for Japan to remain unalterably opposed to sending troops abroad."[8]

This view, known as the Matsudaira statement (*Matsudaira hatsugen*), was assailed by opposition parties, which requested a special Diet session to discuss the issue.[9] Why, they wondered, was a government official advocating the dispatch of troops, when stated policy did not permit it? Even peace-keeping operations involved military contributions, after all. Voicing the apprehensions that Matsudaira's comments aroused in many Japanese people, an editorial in the *Yomiuri Shimbun* linked pressure for SDF participation in UN peace-keeping with a broader LDP effort to revise Article 9. Concern with avoiding the sort of militarism that had characterized Japan prior to World War II is evident: "If the constitution is revised so that troops may be sent abroad there is no knowing when the rightist forces will strengthen their influence and embark on aggression instead of dispatching troops [for peaceful purposes]."[10]

In testimony the following day, Matsudaira argued that he had presented his views as a private citizen, not as an official of MOFA, and that statements to the Council were strictly off the record.[11] He also retracted his statement and emphasized that, irrespective of the purpose, it was MOFA policy to oppose dispatch of the SDF abroad. A few days later, however, Foreign Minister Zentaro Kosaka made sure to emphasize that, although Japan currently was not in a position to consider overseas SDF deployment, decisions on whether or not to send troops abroad in connection with future UN operations should be made in accordance with future conditions.

Despite these rejections, or perhaps because of them, MOFA apparently decided that the only way to resolve the issue of SDF participation was through changes in the legal framework. In February 1966 the *Tokyo Shimbun* revealed that the ministry had drafted a UN Resolutions Cooperation Bill. The bill was divided into two main sections. The first called for full cooperation with economic sanctions mandated under Article 41 of the UN Charter, and was clearly intended as a response to criticisms lodged by the British embassy concerning Japan's adherence to a UN embargo imposed on Southern Rhodesia the previous year.[12] According to the British government, Japanese trading companies had been allowed to continue their business dealings with the illegal regime despite the UN action. More ambitious was the second section, which dealt with Article 42 actions. Here the bill specifically mentioned personnel, *including members of the SDF*, as part of Japan's contribution.[13]

Opposition parties, which did not subscribe to such a policy, moved quickly to determine what the government had in mind. The following day, in a meeting of the Lower House budget committee, an opposition member asked Foreign Minister Etsusaburo Shiina about the newspaper report. Seeking to downplay the bill, the foreign minister indicated that, although dispatching troops was constitutionally permissible, the SDF Law would first need to be revised, because the possibility of the SDF taking part in peace-keeping duties had not been foreseen when the law had been drafted. This, Shiina suggested, would not be an easy matter. As a UN member, however, Japan would need to consider the possibility of a request to send the SDF to join observer groups or other peace-keeping activities. After all, SDF members had the training and expertise necessary to participate in such activities. But Japanese involvement in UN peace-keeping would require investigation, so Japan should not wait until it had received a request but should begin exploring the issue in the near future.[14]

The bill did not make much progress within the government or the LDP. According to one account, it had been considered at the division level of various ministries, and had been discussed by the relevant sections of the LDP Policy Affairs Research Council, but no consensus had been reached and it had not been given much attention among the leadership. Statements made by Defence Agency Director-General Raizo Matsuno indicated that the agency had plans to consider revising the SDF Law, but implied that MOFA had not yet asked the agency to consider the bill. Editorials in the major dailies took the government to task for not coordinating its views on such a sensitive issue. Needless to say, the public uproar ensured that the bill was never brought before the Diet.

These early debates on SDF participation in UN peace-keeping indicate that the political parties had little interest in tackling such a controversial issue. The governing LDP was far more concerned with rebuilding the economy and improving Japan's stature in the international community. The main foreign policy goal was further integration with the global economy, not joining UN actions that could be misinterpreted at home or abroad. MOFA was encouraged to take an active role in the United Nations, a policy that nearly all Japanese strongly supported, but only if military commitments were avoided. That there might be some way to dispatch SDF personnel as part of unarmed observer groups or other actions that did not involve the use of armed force was not appreciated beyond the offices of the ministry. But LDP politicians were persuaded to emphasize Japan's constitutional right to participate in certain UN collective security actions, even if this right could not be exercised. The ministry's goal would be to convince the public and politicians of the need to rectify a fundamental contradiction in its foreign policy, namely that Japan could benefit from a collective security system yet claim exemption from active participation. UN peace-keeping offered a way to resolve this dilemma because it minimized the chances of using force, yet allowed Japan to play a role in supporting international security.

Reconsidering peace-keeping

Events in the late 1960s and early 1970s helped MOFA establish an argument for a more active Japanese role in collective security. To begin with, Japan was recognized as having achieved a high level of economic prosperity, becoming the world's third-largest economy after 1965. At the same time, the declining role of the United States in East Asian security affairs following its withdrawal from Viet Nam suggested that US allies would now have to shoulder a greater portion of the security burden. Many Americans expected Japan to take a leading role in this effort as a way of compensating the United States for its lenient treatment following World War II. Having regained sovereignty over Okinawa and normalized relations with China, many Japanese felt they had settled World War II accounts and were now free to consider new diplomatic horizons.

It was not until the late 1970s that MOFA initiated a new effort to raise its profile in the United Nations. Public opinion and the opposition remained important obstacles. One way of overcoming inertia on security issues was to focus attention on UN peace operations. The government therefore made overtures to those interested in foreign policy questions by creating an advisory group to discuss and report on peace-keeping and other forms of assistance. Such groups are regularly convened by the government as a way of releasing a trial balloon that would help politicians gauge support for policy changes. In the case of dispatching the SDF abroad to peace operations, MOFA was fully aware that the opposition parties remained wary of any plan that involved troops. But, at the same time, international conditions had created a situation in which public opinion might be shifted to support greater Japanese activism, including SDF participation in peace-keeping. Discussing what Japan could do was a necessary first step.

A panel composed of mid-level MOFA bureaucrats was formed in 1979 to discuss Japan's role in international security. The Soviet invasion of Afghanistan had caused great consternation within the ministry, which was already grappling with the threat of the Soviet Pacific fleet. Although a great deal of space was devoted to strengthening US–Japanese military ties, the United Nations was not overlooked, since it offered the least controversial avenue for a Japanese contribution to global security. In July 1980, the group circulated a report declaring that, "with respect to UN peacekeeping activities, a positive discussion should take place on the contribution of personnel in addition to financial cooperation. The dispatch of personnel to UN peacekeeping operations is considered for our country, which desires to exist as a peaceful state."[15] SDF participation was not specifically mentioned, but, given familiarity with government thinking on the matter, opposition Diet members concluded that SDF members would be among the personnel involved.

When Socialist representative Seiichi Inaba asked whether the Japanese government intended to allow the SDF to participate in UN peace-keeping, however, the government responded that, if UN missions entailed the use of armed force (*buryoku koshi wo tomonau*), the dispatch of the SDF was prohibited according to Article 9. If, however, the mission did not entail the use of armed force, the dispatch of the SDF would not be prohibited, though participation in such a mission would require revision of the SDF Law, because UN activities are not mentioned in Article 3 of that law.[16]

Despite the continued resistance of the opposition, the government pursued the issue within the United Nations. In 1982 it submitted to the General Assembly a resolution that "emphasized the need to strengthen the role and effectiveness of the United Nations in maintaining international peace and security. The main feature of this resolution was a plan to set up a body of experts under the authority of the secretary general 'to undertake technical studies regarding the strengthening and expansion of the United Nations peacekeeping functions.' "[17]

Although the resolution was passed by consensus, few countries expressed much interest, and the proposed "committee of experts" was never established. Instead, the United Nations asked individual countries to propose ways to strengthen UN functions. The Japanese government formed an advisory panel under the chairmanship of former UN Ambassador Shizuo Saito, and including prominent academics, among them Sadako Ogata, Shigeru Kozai, and Hidejiro Kotani.[18] The group's final report, delivered directly to the United Nations in September, was divided into two parts. The first contained four general and uncontroversial recommendations: strengthening the UN Security Council, strengthening the office of Secretary-General, strengthening peace-keeping functions, and consideration of regional security issues. The second part dealt with the contributions Japan could make to the United Nations. Here there were seven specific contributions: provision of funds and materials, election supervision, medical assistance, transport and communications activities, police activities, logistical support, and observation and patrol activities.[19]

The report was immediately enveloped in controversy. In the Diet, opposition members demanded to know why MOFA had not submitted the report for their approval or permitted public debate on the proposals. But the fundamental problem was the proposals in the second part of the report. Although the SDF was nowhere mentioned, it was obvious that only SDF personnel had the training and experience to carry out some of the duties mentioned in the report. To the opposition, MOFA was trying to circumvent the Diet and public opinion by announcing to the United Nations that Japan was prepared to send the SDF to UN peace-keeping operations. The government, of course, saw it differently: Japan should contribute personnel to UN activities, especially those related to global security. Participation in certain peace-keeping operations was permitted under the constitution and Japan ought to consider this option. The UN report was meant to spark discussion not circumvent it. But, as a result of the ensuing criticism both in the Diet and in the Japanese press, MOFA decided to re-submit a version of the report that omitted the second part.[20] Prime Minister Nakasone publicly dismissed the report, calling it "merely one view put forward by a private study group," and reiterated his government's adherence to the long-standing official view, namely that there could be no SDF participation in UN operations if the use of armed force was contemplated.[21] Once again, public pressure had forced the government to retreat.

MOFA had clearly attempted to forge a new foreign policy that envisioned Japan as a more active player in UN affairs as a way of expanding its contribution to the international community. The opposition parties and the public remained suspicious of where this new course might lead Japan. But the real question was, did the MOFA initiative make any difference? Arguably not. The problem was, as MOFA official Takahiro Shinyo put it, that "it did not really matter whether we [Japan] did nothing or whether the U.N. did not function; the world danced to the tune of the rivalry between the United States and the Soviet Union."[22] Until these tensions subsided, the United Nations could not play a major role in resolving global conflict, and, unless the United Nations played such a role, Japan's initiatives would make little difference.

Takeshita's initiative: Responding to a reinvigorated United Nations

The waning of East–West conflict succeeded where efforts by Japan and other countries to reinvigorate the United Nations had failed. Suddenly the organization was able – and expected – to play a role in conflict management. And the implication of the revival of the United Nations was not lost on MOFA. The ministry knew that Japan would be expected to take part in helping the United Nations overcome the difficulties the organization now confronted. Certainly an increased financial contribution was possible, but by the mid-1980s Japan was already providing more money than any other country except the United States. The other possibility was to establish a visible presence in UN peace-keeping. Since no Japanese had been involved in these operations, which were rapidly gaining a great deal of international attention, MOFA felt that sending Japanese personnel on such missions would strengthen Japan's diplomatic voice. However, to avoid any potential political controversy, the ministry was at first content to send government officials, not SDF personnel, to participate in UN peace-keeping operations.[23]

A major breakthrough came when Noboru Takeshita became prime minister in

November 1987. Takeshita, building on the work of Nakasone, took concrete steps to expand Japan's involvement in international affairs. As part of his efforts, he proposed the International Cooperation Initiative in 1988 and identified five areas in which Japan was to play a larger role: active pursuit of diplomatic efforts aimed at strengthening political dialogue and international cooperation; stepped-up contributions for UN-sponsored activities seeking to prevent outbreak of conflicts; active involvement in international efforts to resolve disputes peacefully (such as dispatching civilian personnel to trouble-spots to assist with the supervision of elections or provide transportation, communications, or medical services); strengthened assistance to refugees through both bilateral and multilateral efforts; and vigorous contributions – in terms of both money and personnel – to international cooperative efforts aimed at reconstruction once a conflict is peacefully resolved.[24]

Takeshita immediately began steering Japan toward a more active role in UN peace-keeping and related activities. MOFA was already busy arranging to send an official to the UN mission to mediate between Afghanistan and Pakistan (UN Good Offices Mission in Afghanistan and Pakistan, or UNGOMAP) and sent another to the team monitoring the Iran–Iraq cease-fire (the UN Iran–Iraq Military Observer Group, or UNIIMOG) in 1988. In 1989, 31 Japanese personnel (including 19 officials from regional public corporations) were sent to Namibia (UN Transition Assistance Group, or UNTAG) to monitor elections and in 1990 six went to Nicaragua (UN Observation Mission for Elections in Nicaragua, or ONUVEN). Although the opposition parties were sceptical of the intent behind these efforts, there was little to argue with – the government did have the right to dispatch civilians abroad and these civilians were performing duties under UN auspices for humanitarian purposes.

By 1990, MOFA had succeeded in establishing a presence, albeit a minimal one, in UN peace-keeping missions. This had been accomplished with little fanfare, however, because dispatch of ministry officials was permissible under Japanese law. Having got its foot in the door, MOFA now faced the more difficult hurdle of convincing the public and the opposition parties that military personnel ought to be included. Although government personnel could be sent to observe elections or to handle administrative duties, they would not have the necessary training for monitoring cease-fires or coping with other risky situations. Realistically, the only choice was to dispatch SDF personnel, who had the requisite experience to handle peace-keeping duties under adverse conditions. Despite these reasons, opposition parties continued to view participation in UN peace-keeping as part of a Machiavellian strategy by conservatives to expand Japan's military role abroad. It was also unclear whether public attitudes toward the SDF had changed, despite a gradual decline in polarization over defence and security issues. Although there was support for the SDF mission of defending Japan, the majority of Japanese remained leery of dispatching forces abroad.[25]

The turning point

The Persian Gulf crisis and war sparked a nationwide debate on Japan's role in global security affairs, serving as the catalyst for efforts that ultimately led to active participation in UN peace-keeping operations. When Iraq invaded Kuwait in August 1990, the Japanese government responded by supporting economic sanctions against Iraq and providing generous financial assistance both to countries affected by the invasion and to the multinational coalition forces protecting Saudi Arabia. Under pressure from the United States, it also made efforts to secure passage of a bill that would allow the SDF to provide logistical support for the US-led forces, in addition to participating in traditional peace-keeping operations. But a majority of Japanese – including many members of the governing LDP – came to believe that, under the provisions of this bill, SDF personnel could become involved in the use of military force, a violation of Article 9. As a result, the legislation was withdrawn and Japanese military personnel played no part in either the crisis or the war.

The failure to provide military personnel provoked strong criticism from the United States and some European countries. Japan was accused of resorting to "chequebook diplomacy" in order to avoid "sweating" with the coalition forces. At the conclusion of the Persian Gulf war, Kuwait pointedly excluded Japan from a full-page advertisement in the *New York Times* thanking those countries that had provided assistance. A sense of impotence mixed with embarrassment and irritation led to a reconsideration of Japan's role in global security. The decision to dispatch a flotilla of minesweepers to the Persian Gulf – a decision that had substantial public support – indicated that the Japanese government was no longer content with a passive role in international security.

At the same time, the government set to work in early 1991 on a new bill to permit SDF participation in UN peace-keeping operations. MOFA was especially concerned that this legislation not be a victim of domestic politics. In Cambodia, there were signs that a resolution of the decade-long conflict was in the offing, and the ministry, which had been increasingly involved in the international negotiations on the Cambodia question, wanted Japan to play a key role in the UN peace-keeping operation that would commence once a formal agreement had been reached. More than the criticism of Japan during the Persian Gulf crisis, the desire to play a part in the UN Transitional Authority in Cambodia (UNTAC) was the main impetus behind the ministry's efforts. With the signing of the Paris Accords in October, just after the new bill was submitted to the Diet, these efforts gained increased urgency.

In addition, the end of East–West tensions had raised the prospect of expanding the number of permanent seats on the UN Security Council to reflect changes in the international system. Given Japan's large financial contribution and its general enthusiasm for the United Nations, the ministry felt that the country deserved to have one of the new seats. The single drawback was its reluctance to participate in UN collective security actions. Passing the peace-keeping legislation and sending the SDF to Cambodia and other operations would go some way toward mitigating criticism that, as a permanent member of the Security Council, Japan would be asked to vote on security issues in which it could not participate.

In order to gain support from centrist parties, which would be crucial for passage of the bill in the Diet, the governing LDP was forced to make numerous concessions.[26] Most of these were designed to ensure that Japanese personnel did not become involved in armed conflicts. To begin with, the SDF would be allowed to join only those peace-keeping operations in which certain specified conditions – a cease-fire must be in effect, the belligerent parties must agree to UN and Japanese participation, UN personnel must remain impartial in carrying out the mission – had been satisfied. SDF members would be permitted to carry out a wide range of tasks but, if the government wanted to send lightly armed SDF units to handle assignments such as patrolling buffer zones, it would first need to seek Diet approval.[27] While in the field, Japanese military personnel would be expected to operate according to rules of engagement that allowed them to use weapons only in strict self-defence. If conditions in the host country deteriorated, personnel were to be immediately withdrawn.

Deliberations on this bill extended across three often-stormy Diet sessions. As in the past, arguments for and against sending the SDF abroad were based on very different interpretations of Article 9. The Social Democratic Party of Japan (formerly the Japan Socialist Party) claimed that, even with the additional safeguards, the bill violated the spirit of Article 9 in that armed Japanese soldiers would be setting foot on foreign soil. The LDP, meanwhile, claimed that a distinction could be made between sending the SDF abroad with the intention of using force, and sending the SDF abroad to participate in UN peace-keeping or humanitarian operations. The latter, the LDP, argued was well within the parameters of the official interpretation of Article 9.

On 15 June 1992, the LDP and its political allies finally managed to push the legislation through the Diet and two months later the Law Concerning Cooperation for United Nations Peace-keeping Operations and Other Operations (hereafter referred to as the Peace-keeping Law) went into effect. Since then, the Japanese government has been able to dispatch the SDF abroad to three peace-keeping operations (in Cambodia, Mozambique, and the Golan Heights) and to one humanitarian operation to aid Rwandan refugees in eastern Zaire. Despite the new law, however, the decision-making process remained contentious, as progressive political forces subjected each proposed dispatch to intense scrutiny in order to ensure that Japan could not be accused of using armed force. As a result, the prospects for expanding SDF participation remain unclear.

Notes

1. UN document S/4055/rev 1.
2. For details, see Hidejiro Kotani, "Jietai no kaigai haken to kokuren kyoryoku," *Boei Ronshu*, vol. 2, no. 1, 1963, pp. 24–41, esp. 30–34.
3. An article in the *Sankei Shimbun*, 3 August 1958, indicated that officials from the Cabinet Legal Affairs Bureau, MOFA, and the Defence Agency had agreed that dispatching SDF officers to UNOGIL was both constitutional and legal. See also the report of Director-General Sato's testimony before the Upper House Cabinet Committee in *Asahi Shimbun*, 30 September 1958.
4. *Yomiuri Shimbun*, evening edition, 2 August 1958.
5. *Asahi Shimbun*, 3 August 1958.
6. This mission was also among the most costly in terms of fatalities, leading to the deaths of 195 members, including Hammarskjöld, who perished in a plane crash.
7. *Asahi Shimbun*, 28 January 1961.
8. *Asahi Shimbun*, 22 February 1961.
9. The Democratic Socialists had split off from the Japan Socialist Party in 1960.

10. *Yomiuri Shimbun*, 23 February 1961.
11. The *Asahi Janaru*, however, suggested that Matsudaira's views were not those of an isolated individual, but reflected widespread dissatisfaction in the government and LDP (vol. 3, no. 10, 5 March 1961, p. 77).
12. Southern Rhodesia had unilaterally declared independence in November 1965. A subsequent UN Security Council resolution called on members to refrain from all actions that would assist the illegal regime and to do their utmost to break all economic relations with it.
13. *Tokyo Shimbun*, 23 February 1965.
14. Hidejiro Kotani, "Jieitai wa kaigai hahei dekiru ka," *Jiyu*, May 1966, p. 22.
15. *Asahi Shimbun*, 28 July 1980, provides the gist of the report.
16. Tsurutani has argued that this interpretation injected a significant element of ambiguity into the issue of whether or not the government was permitted to dispatch forces, but a review of earlier policy statements suggests that it was merely a reiteration of the standard government interpretation. Taketsugu Tsurutani, *Japanese Policy and East Asian Security*, Boulder, CO: Praeger, 1981, p. 170.
17. Sadako Ogata, "The United Nations and Japanese diplomacy," *Japan Review of International Affairs*, Fall/Winter 1990, p. 149. The inner quotation is from Japan's *note verbale* to the United Nations on 25 June 1982.
18. On the activities of this panel, see Sadako Ogata, op. cit. (note 17), p. 159; Shigeru Kozai, *Kokuren no Heiwa Iji Katsudo*, Tokyo: Yuhikaku, 1991, pp. 501–503.
19. *Asahi Shimbun*, 19 September 1983.
20. Interview with Professor Shigeru Kozai, September 1994; see also *Yomiuri Shimbun*, 23 September 1983 and 29 December 1994.
21. *Nihon Keizai Shimbun*, 19 September 1983, evening edition.
22. Takahiro Shinyo, "The conditions of permanent membership in the United Nations," *Japan Echo*, vol. XXI, no. 2, Summer 1993, p. 58.
23. The absence of Japanese civilian personnel was not due to any legal restriction; in 1974 Foreign Minister Ohira had mentioned the possibility of sending government officials, other than those connected with the Defence Agency or SDF, to participate in UN peace-keeping activities. See records of the 72nd Diet, House of Representatives, Foreign Affairs Committee, 24 May 1974.
24. Barbara Wanner, "Persian Gulf crisis tests limits of Japan's foreign policy," *JEL Report*, no. 6A, 15 February 1991, p. 4.
25. An opinion poll taken by the Prime Minister's Office in early 1989 pointed up the ambivalence in public attitudes. On the question of sending the SDF abroad to participate in UN peace-keeping, 46.5 per cent of respondents were opposed, while only 22.4 per cent were in favour. Yet the survey also showed that 72.2 per cent were prepared to send the SDF abroad for the purpose of disaster rescue operations, compared with only 19.9 per cent who opposed such duties.

26. The LDP had lost its majority in the House of Councillors (the Upper House) in the July 1989 election. Under the constitution, the LDP could secure passage of a bill without the approval of the House of Councillors, but this required the support of two-thirds of the membership of the House of Representatives (the Lower House).

27. This provision was later frozen. For details, see chapter 6.

2

RECENT GOVERNMENT

POLICY

Since 1992 the Japanese government has been cautiously exercising its new authority to dispatch the Self-Defence Forces to UN peace operations. As noted in the previous chapter, the Ministry of Foreign Affairs had been keen to participate in the UN Transitional Authority in Cambodia (UNTAC) and wasted little time proposing that a contingent be sent to Cambodia. On 8 September, just weeks after the Peace-keeping Law had gone into effect, the cabinet approved the dispatch of 600 SDF engineers to Takeo Province and 8 military observers to sites throughout the country. In addition, 75 policemen were to be sent to UNTAC's Civilian Police (CIVPOL) unit. This was the first and, to date, largest deployment of military personnel since the end of World War II.

In so far as UNTAC's mission can be judged a success, Japan can rightfully claim a share of the credit. At the same time, however, Japanese participation was not without difficulties. Although the engineers performed their assigned duties expertly, SDF field commanders had little flexibility to handle ad hoc requests for their assistance. Worried that they would be accused of overstepping their mandate and subjected to intense scrutiny by hundreds of Japanese reporters, commanders felt they had no choice but to request government approval any time the SDF was asked to perform duties that were even slightly different from those listed in the Implementation Plan. The government, which was equally concerned about possible violations of the Peace-keeping Law, was usually slow to respond, which meant that the SDF was rarely able to offer assistance beyond its specified tasks. The inflexibility of Japanese units was irritating to Cambodians and UN personnel in need of such assistance.

The safety of Japanese personnel was a far more serious concern to the government, which had argued that the safeguards incorporated into the Peace-keeping Law would ensure that the SDF handled only non-combat duties. But, in Cambodia, the government was faced with a situation in which one faction, the Khmer Rouge, was refusing to act in accordance with the terms of the peace settlement. Although never officially repudiating the terms, the Khmer Rouge would not lay down its weapons and skirmishes continued, leading many to question whether a cease-fire was truly in effect. Even in Takeo Province, one of the least dangerous areas, SDF personnel were nearly involved in several armed clashes. In Japan, the Socialists and Communists called for the withdrawal of SDF and other Japanese personnel.

As the 1993 national elections neared, the violence increased as the Khmer Rouge threatened to disrupt the voting. At this point, two incidents led the Japanese government to consider a withdrawal. In April, a young Japanese UN volunteer was killed in mysterious circumstances and, a few weeks later, a Japanese policeman was killed when he and some Dutch CIVPOL members were ambushed by the Khmer Rouge. The Japanese public, who had assumed UN peace operations to be non-violent, were stunned by these deaths. Leaders from both sides of the political spectrum attacked the government's failure to protect Japanese personnel and demanded that they be either moved to safer locations or withdrawn. The International Peace Cooperation Headquarters (IPCHQ), the Japanese government agency that handles matters pertaining to UN peace operations, requested that Japanese policemen in dangerous locales be transferred, but to no avail. To its credit, the government rejected demands to withdraw personnel, arguing that both Japan's international reputation and the Cambodian recovery were at stake.

To ensure the safety of Japanese personnel, the government took a controversial step and assigned the SDF a more overt security role. Worried about Japanese working at polling stations, groups of lightly armed SDF members would be allowed to visit polling stations for the purpose of gathering information. The announcement led to vociferous protests in the Diet that armed SDF soldiers would be patrolling the polling stations in order to guard against Khmer Rouge attacks, a violation of the Peace-keeping Law. Fortunately for the government and the SDF, however, the Khmer Rouge allowed the election to proceed and Japan suffered no further casualties.

Japanese participation in UNTAC was an important first step for MOFA and the IPCHQ, but it had been relatively easy to generate support and enthusiasm for the Cambodian operation because Japan had a strong interest in South-East Asian affairs and numerous ties with the region. The next challenge would be to send the SDF to an operation outside Japan's normal sphere of interest.

The first opportunity came in late 1992, as SDF engineers began their duties in Takeo Province. On the other side of the Indian Ocean, the United States had begun flying in supplies to Somalia, a country on the verge of complete political and economic collapse. When warring factions made it risky for international relief workers to aid starving Somalis, US President George Bush proposed sending troops with a mandate from the United Nations to use force to ensure that aid reached those who needed it. In December, the UN Security Council approved the formation of a Unified Task Force (UNITAF) under US leadership. MOFA was keen on making a contribution, perhaps recalling the situation in the Persian Gulf two years before, and did briefly consider sending the SDF. However, owing to the deteriorating political circumstances in Somalia, there was little chance that the warring factions would agree to a formal cease-fire, which meant that the SDF could not be sent under the Peace-keeping Law. The ministry also had trouble providing financial assistance to Japanese NGOs, most of which had left the country because of the increasing risks.

Although Somalia was out of the question, MOFA began to take an interest in Mozambique, where a peace accord had been reached and a UN peace-keeping operation (UN Operation in Mozambique, or ONUMOZ) was set to begin. Upon investigating the situation, the IPCHQ found that all of the important conditions for dispatching the SDF had been met: a cease-fire was in effect and both the domestic factions had agreed to a UN presence. In early 1993, the IPCHQ proposed sending SDF personnel, but initially the Miyazawa government was not interested, since it was already involved in Cambodia. But, with some public prodding from UN Secretary-General Boutros Ghali, it eventually decided to participate and sent a 53-person contingent to handle movement control duties.

Japan's participation in ONUMOZ lasted from May 1993 until December

1995 and attracted far less attention than the unit sent to Cambodia. Not only did few Japanese have an interest in, or knowledge of, affairs in Mozambique, but the operation was relatively safe. Although there was friction between the two domestic political rivals, and elections were postponed on two occasions, Japanese personnel were apparently never in danger. Lacking an element of risk and located in a region that had little relevance for Japan, the Mozambique mission was largely ignored.

MOFA also considered taking part in the UN Protection Force (UNPROFOR) established in the former Yugoslavia. In the last weeks of 1993, both the newly appointed head of UNPROFOR, Yasushi Akashi, and UN Secretary-General Boutros Ghali appealed to the Japanese government for SDF personnel. Although most of the area was in turmoil, the United Nations was planning a preventive deployment on the border between Macedonia and Serbia, where the situation was stable, and the IPCHQ felt that a case could be made for SDF participation there. In Japan, however, domestic political factors worked against participation. The previous summer, the long-governing Liberal Democrats had been replaced by a loose coalition of eight political groups, including the Japan Socialist Party, which had opposed SDF participation. Since the main goal of the coalition was to push through controversial political reforms, it could not afford to consider a proposal that would antagonize the Socialists, and so Japan did not send the SDF to Macedonia.

In the summer of 1994, however, an opportunity arose for Japan to participate in its first humanitarian relief operation under the Peace-keeping Law. An ethnic conflict in Rwanda had forced thousands of refugees to flee to neighbouring countries, where they had insufficient food, water, and sanitation. To deal with the growing tragedy, the UN High Commissioner for Refugees (UNHCR) was overseeing a massive relief operation that included both military and civilian personnel. The UNHCR director, Sadako Ogata, made a direct appeal to Japan and, after a month of discussions, the government finally agreed to send the SDF to assist in the effort. This came as something of a surprise because, by this time, a coalition of Liberal Democrats and Socialists, former rivals, was in power and the first Socialist prime minister in nearly 50 years now headed the cabinet. But the Socialist Party was in the process of adopting a far more moderate position on military matters and had decided that dispatching the SDF to humanitarian relief operations was a beneficial contribution to global welfare.

Although the 283-person SDF contingent arrived after the worst of the tragedy was over, it did provide a number of vital services and its lightly armed soldiers were a reassuring presence, since almost all other military contingents had departed. As in Cambodia, the safety of Japanese personnel was a major concern because, interspersed with the refugee population, were remnants of the Rwandan government army that had disintegrated during the domestic conflict. The former soldiers, most of whom had weapons, were prepared to use violence to get food and other supplies. Neither the Japanese government nor the SDF was fully aware of the potential dangers the refugee camps posed, and a number of politicians were angered by the failure of IPCHQ and MOFA to provide them with adequate information. None the less, the SDF contingent returned to Japan without serious mishap.

In the early months of 1994, the IPCHQ began to give serious consideration to sending SDF personnel to the UN Disengagement Observer Force (UNDOF) in the Golan Heights. MOFA saw participation in a Middle East peace-keeping operation as a way to augment the substantial financial aid it provided to countries in the region, thereby raising Japan's political visibility. Moreover, because UNDOF had strong support from both Israel and Syria, there seemed little likelihood of major risks to the safety of Japanese personnel. The only problem was that the disengagement force was already fully subscribed by peace-keepers from other countries. Fortunately for Japan, the Canadian government was under some financial pressure to reduce its peace-keeping obligations and was therefore amenable to a plan by which SDF personnel would replace a portion of a Canadian logistics unit that handled transportation of supplies. In this case, Japan asked to participate in a peace-keeping operation prior to the request issued by the United Nations.

Japanese domestic politics once again proved to be a major obstacle to sending the SDF abroad, however. When the IPCHQ approached the governing coalition with the proposal, Socialist members raised objections over the potential dangers of having SDF personnel handle transport duties. In a crisis, they pointed out, SDF drivers might be asked to carry ammunition or armed soldiers, which under Japanese law could be considered tantamount to using force and therefore prohibited by the constitution. An additional concern was that the head of UNDOF wanted Japan to commit to a two-year stint, which some felt could undermine the government's right to withdraw the SDF if trouble arose. For these and a variety of other reasons, a decision on participating in the Golan Heights operation was delayed for over a year before the government was finally able to reach agreement.

In August 1995 the coalition parties finally negotiated a compromise. In order to ensure that SDF personnel did not become entangled in conflict, they would not be allowed to transport ammunition or foreign combat troops, nor would they be permitted to join UN training exercises in which live ammunition was used. On the basis of this agreement, a 45-person SDF contingent arrived in the Golan Heights in February 1996 on a two-year mission.

As should be abundantly clear, Japan's participation in UN peace operations since 1992 continues to be undertaken with caution and deliberation. Although the public generally support the Peace-keeping Law, they are also very concerned that SDF personnel sent to peace-keeping operations not be involved in combat. With some notable exceptions, the positions of the major political parties on peace-keeping reflect this concern. As a result, decisions on dispatching the SDF consume a great deal of time and effort, as officials from the IPCHQ and MOFA labour to convince politicians that the risks to Japanese personnel are minimal. Politicians, particularly Socialist members, subject each proposal to intense scrutiny in order to ensure that the conditions of the Peace-keeping Law are met to the letter.

Having finally managed to secure a minor role in UN peace operations, elements within the Japanese government have been seeking to relax the numerous constraints that inhibit Japan's ability to take part in a wider range of operations. The focus of their efforts is the Peace-keeping Law, which, as noted in chapter 4, includes a provision mandating a review of the law. In the review process, various revisions to the law were to be considered in light of the SDF's experiences in peace operations during the three-year period beginning August 1992. Well before the process got under way, certain aspects of the law had already been flagged by the IPCHQ for review, including the ban on the dispatch of peace-keeping forces (the PKF freeze) and the five principles. Lifting the freeze or modifying the principles would allow the government to send the SDF to a wider range of missions.

In August 1996, the director general of the IPCHQ presented to the chief cabinet secretary a list of desirable, albeit modest, revisions to the Peace-keeping Law.[1] The first is designed to align Japan's weapons-use policy with standard

UN operating procedures. Under the proposal, SDF personnel would be able use their weapons on the orders of the unit commander to defend themselves as well as non-SDF personnel. Although there has never been any suggestion that SDF personnel would not follow orders given by a commanding officer or stand idly by while other UN personnel were attacked, the discrepancy in the Japanese and UN weapons-use policies has been a potential source of confusion should an emergency arise. Even if the revision were approved, Japanese peace-keepers would still be restricted in comparison with peace-keepers from other countries, because the law does not explicitly allow SDF personnel "to defend the UN mission."[2]

A second proposed revision involves providing material assistance to humanitarian missions. Under the current law, in order to provide assistance to any peace operation, whether peace-keeping or humanitarian, the same conditions apply; i.e. there must be a cease-fire in effect and the belligerent parties must agree to the presence of UN personnel. When the Japanese government is contemplating the dispatch of SDF personnel, these conditions are meaningful and reflect public concerns. In the case of material assistance, these same conditions are annoying obstacles that prevent Japan from offering food and supplies. Since humanitarian relief operations may be conducted in states that have collapsed, finding an official to sanction the operation may be impossible.

Surprisingly, nothing was said about lifting the restrictions on dispatching "peace-keeping forces" to patrol buffer zones and other infantry missions. When proposals for changing the law were first discussed in the Summer of 1994, the most prominent item was ending the PKF freeze. It may be that the difficulties experienced in carrying out UN peace enforcement missions have bolstered the arguments of those Japanese who oppose participation in more risky operations. But, even if the freeze were to be lifted at some future date, it would merely offer the possibility of having the SDF carry out a wider range of traditional peace-keeping duties. Because Diet approval would be required before peace-keeping forces could be dispatched, there is no guarantee that Japanese participation in UN peace-keeping operations would be significantly expanded.

In early March 1997, Taku Yamazaki, the head of the LDP's Policy Research Affairs Council, and a prominent advocate of SDF participation in UN peace-keeping, stated that, although the revision of the Peace-keeping Law was important for Japan, it was not a matter that had to be dealt with in the current Diet session. He pointed out that, given the state of UN peace-keeping missions (presumably he meant that enthusiasm for peace-keeping had been ebbing in recent years), revisions to the law were not urgent, and indicated that issues such as the disposition of US military bases on Okinawa and conditions on the Korean peninsula required the full attention of the governing coalition. The timing for proposing these revisions before the Diet will thus depend on domestic political circumstances.[3]

In addition to revising the Peace-keeping Law, Ichiro Ozawa and other conservative politicians have favoured revising Article 9 of the constitution in order to make clear their contention that Japan fulfil all rights and duties of UN membership, including military participation in actions approved by the UN Security Council. In November 1994, the *Yomiuri Shimbun*, the Japanese daily with the largest circulation, made a public call for revision and published its own version of a new Japanese constitution. But, despite recent opinion polls indicating that the public also favour revising Article 9, it will require a great deal of time and effort. To begin with, although many want to amend Article 9, it is equally apparent that there is not yet a consensus on how it should be changed. Moderates, for example, would support a clause that makes clear that the SDF is constitutional, but probably would oppose any dilution of the prohibition on using military force abroad, as hardliners have proposed. Another difficulty is the amendment process itself. In order to ratify an amendment, it must have the support of two-thirds of the membership in each Diet chamber, and garner a majority of all votes cast in a national referendum.

Two external factors are likely to have an influence on the shape of Japanese policy in the future. The first is the current effort to strengthen US–Japanese security ties so as to manage regional security better in the post–Cold War period. One area that both countries have considered in their recent efforts to revise the Guidelines for US–Japan Defense Cooperation is joint participation in UN peace-keeping operations. Working with the US military under the US–Japan Mutual Security Treaty has obvious political advantages for Japanese leaders because the public support the treaty. In addition, access to US sea- and air-lift capabilities would be especially helpful for the SDF, which has a limited number of large transport aircraft and ships.

The second factor is the current effort to reform the UN Security Council in order to reflect changes in the international system since 1945. Most proposals call for the expansion in the number of permanent members from the present five (the United States, the United Kingdom, France, China, and Russia), but differ radically with respect to how many members the new Security Council would have and whether the new members would have veto power. As the second-largest contributor to the United Nations and the largest source of foreign aid, Japan naturally believes it has a claim to one of the new permanent seats, but so too do a number of other countries and it is not clear when the matter will be resolved.[4] If a proposal is eventually passed by the UN General Assembly and Japan does join the Security Council, MOFA may argue that, as a permanent member, Japan must modify the restrictions on the SDF in order to expand its participation in UN collective security actions. Japanese political leaders and the general public could well be swayed by this argument, given the country's enhanced international prestige.

Notes

1. *Asahi Shimbun*, 26 August and 6 September 1996.
2. For example, according to UNDOF standard operating procedures, UN peace-keepers are allowed to use their weapons against those who obstruct the UNDOF mission. In theory, Japanese peace-keepers would not be able to take part in these efforts.
3. *Nihon Keizai Shimbun*, 4 March 1997.
4. On 20 March 1997, the UN General Assembly President, Razali Ismail of Malaysia, proposed adding five permanent members but without veto powers. Two would be advanced industrial countries, and the other three would come from Africa, Asia, and Latin America.

3

THE DECISION-MAKING PROCESS

In this chapter we examine the process by which the Japanese government decides to dispatch the Self-Defence Forces (SDF) and other personnel to UN peace operations. Since the passage of the Peace-keeping Law, Japan has dispatched the SDF to operations in Cambodia, Mozambique, Zaire, and the Golan Heights, but it has also declined UN requests to send troops to operations in Somalia and the former Yugoslavia.[1] In either case, the decision-making process begins with private negotiations between the United Nations and the International Peace Cooperation Headquarters (IPCHQ), the Japanese government agency that handles matters pertaining to UN peace operations. In the majority of cases, the United Nations informs the IPCHQ that a peace operation is to be established and requests Japanese participation, although, as noted in chapter 2, Japan approached the United Nations in the case of the Golan Heights operation.

Once the IPCHQ has begun to consider participation in a UN peace operation, the initial task is to make a preliminary determination whether an operation meets the conditions imposed by Japanese law. Specifically, IPCHQ officials must be certain that a cease-fire is in effect, that the belligerent parties have agreed to UN and Japanese participation, and that the United Nations intends to maintain strict impartiality. In many instances, the IPCHQ will rule out SDF participation at this early stage, as it did with proposals to send personnel to Somalia and the former Yugoslavia.

If, on the other hand, the IPCHQ determines that an operation meets the necessary conditions, it then forwards the proposal to the influential chief cabinet
secretary, who is charged with coordinating government policy among all ministries and agencies. The chief cabinet secretary must gauge whether the proposal
will garner sufficient political support to overcome domestic opposition, which is
often considerable. The mass media, the public, opinion leaders, and progressive
politicians are certain to scrutinize each proposal to ensure that the government
has carefully weighed the risks to Japanese personnel and is not allowing the
SDF to perform duties beyond those provided for in the Peace-keeping Law.
This stage is easily the most sensitive and time consuming of the entire decision-
making process.

If a proposal meets with political approval, the IPCHQ then proposes that a
fact-finding mission be dispatched to the country in which the peace operation
will take place. The fact-finding team makes a final determination on whether the
conditions set forth in the Peace-keeping Law have been met and reports to the
Diet. The first three teams were composed mainly of government officials, but
some politicians felt that they were not receiving adequate information. As a
result, a fact-finding team composed of politicians went to the Golan Heights in
April 1995 in order to provide an alternative source of information. Assuming
the fact-finding mission has no major objections, the chief cabinet secretary
issues a preparatory statement informing all cabinet members that the proposed
mission meets the preconditions set forth in the Peace-keeping Law and asks
their ministries and agencies to provide the necessary cooperation.

At this point, the IPCHQ will be directed to begin drawing up an Implementation Plan (*jisshi keikaku*) for cabinet consideration. The plan describes the
duties SDF personnel will perform, the length of time they will be overseas, the
types of weapons they will be allowed to carry, and other important details of
Japanese participation. When the plan has been drafted, the IPCHQ contacts the
United Nations and asks that a formal request for Japanese participation be
issued. In most cases the UN request also includes a message from the host
country inviting Japan to send the SDF. Once the Japanese government has
received the UN request, the cabinet formally votes to approve the Implementation Plan and the SDF begins preparations to send personnel abroad.

To date, the decision-making process has been both cumbersome and time
consuming. In the cases of Cambodia and Zaire, it took the government about

four weeks to reach agreement on sending the SDF abroad, Mozambique required about three months, and the Golan Heights about a year and a half. So far, the inability to reach a quick decision has had few major political costs although, by the time the cabinet approved sending the SDF to eastern Zaire in 1994, most of the major duties had already been assigned to peace-keepers from other countries or NGOs, somewhat lessening the value of the Japanese contribution.

The government

The Ministry of Foreign Affairs (MOFA) plays a key role in any decision to send the SDF to participate in peace operations. As mentioned, the ministry has a strong interest in having Japan take part in such operations. Sending the SDF abroad may improve Japan's chances of gaining a permanent seat on the UN Security Council, is the most politically acceptable way to contribute to inter-national security, and reassures other countries that Japan is a positive force in global affairs. MOFA has several ways of influencing the decision-making pro-cess. First a MOFA official always occupies the post of deputy director of the IPCHQ, allowing the ministry to initiate and supervise the decision-making pro-cess. Secondly, the Peace-keeping Law gives the Minister of Foreign Affairs the right to request the prime minister to propose a peace-keeping operation to the cabinet. Thirdly, with the exception of fact-finding missions, the ministry is the primary source of information on conditions in countries hosting peace oper-ations, which means that other decision makers must rely on the MOFA.

The Japanese military establishment – the civilian Defence Agency and the uniformed Self-Defence Forces – has far less influence on the decision-making process than the military establishments of other countries. The abiding suspicion of the military that arose after World War II has created strong support for constraints on the Defence Agency that prevent it from having a major impact on policy-making. Not only is the Defence Agency not a full-fledged ministry but a number of important positions within the agency are filled by officials seconded from other ministries. On the other hand, because SDF personnel are sent to participate in UN peace operations, it is critical to have a military view-point. Defence Agency officials are among IPCHQ staff and are always part of fact-finding teams, while SDF officers are regularly consulted on military matters.

The Defence Agency has a decidedly mixed view on SDF participation in UN peace operations. On the one hand, the agency is first and foremost concerned with the defence of Japanese territory against external attack. To the extent that its personnel and equipment are diverted for use in UN peace operations, the agency is concerned that it may be unable to provide an adequate level of defence. On the other hand, the agency is also concerned with domestic public perceptions of the SDF. Since the SDF was established in 1954, the agency has spent a great deal of time and money cultivating a more positive image of Japanese soldiers. To the extent that participation in UN peace operations translates into increased public support for the SDF, which was clearly true in Cambodia and Zaire, the Defence Agency sees UN peace operations as working in its favour.

By virtue of his roles as head of the cabinet, commander-in-chief of the SDF, and director of the IPCHQ, the prime minister is clearly positioned to have a major influence on UN peace operations. But, in the period since the Peace-keeping Law was passed in 1992, those men elected prime minister have had more important issues to manage, and so have chosen to downplay or ignore this sensitive issue. The single exception was LDP Prime Minister Kiichi Miyazawa (1991–1993), who expended a great deal of political capital to support SDF participation in Cambodia, even as conditions in the country deteriorated and risks to Japanese personnel increased. Partly because of the difficulties in Cambodia, Miyazawa evinced little interest in sending the SDF to Mozambique until pressured by the UN Secretary-General and members of his own party. During the tenure of Morihiro Hosokawa and Tsutomu Hata (1993–1994), who led the coalition of parties that replaced the LDP, the overriding concern was political reform, so neither could afford to give much attention to peace operations. Under Socialist Prime Minister Tomiichi Murayama (1994–1996), Japan sent the SDF to the Rwanda refugee relief operation and to the Golan Heights. But Murayama and his fellow Socialists were extremely cautious in their approach to UN peace operations. Their concern over sending the SDF to the Golan Heights was an important reason it took well over a year to reach agreement on this proposal.

Political parties

One of the critical aspects in the decision-making process is whether the IPCHQ can convince the political leaders to agree to dispatch the SDF abroad. Within the Japanese political system, there is little incentive for politicians strongly to support military issues, so it is necessary for the IPCHQ to present a strong case that SDF participation will not cause a public opinion backlash. In addition, we must keep in mind that sending the SDF abroad is never the only item on the political agenda. Since 1992, the pressing needs arising as a result of the economic slump, political corruption, the Kobe earthquake, and the banking crisis have taken priority over UN peace operations. Perhaps it is not surprising that politicians do not reach quick decisions on military matters.

When the Peace-keeping Law was passed in 1992, the Liberal Democratic Party (LDP) had a majority in the House of Representatives (or Lower House) and therefore controlled the government, as it had done since 1955. The LDP was basically pro-military, though it was possible to distinguish between moderates such as Kiichi Miyazawa and Yohei Kono, and hardliners such as Ichiro Ozawa, Takeo Nishioka, and Taku Yamazaki. Moderates were cautious about sending the SDF abroad and satisfied with the restrictions imposed by the Peace-keeping Law, whereas the hardliners wanted the SDF to participate in a wide range of UN peace operations and hoped to revise the law in order to fulfil all UN collective security obligations.

The progressive Japan Socialist Party (JSP) and Japan Communist Party both opposed dispatching the SDF abroad for any reason, seeing this as a first step toward remilitarization. But, as opposition parties, they had only an indirect influence on the decision-making process. One way of demonstrating their disfavour was by employing various tactics to stall the legislative process. Although dispatching the SDF abroad was not voted on in the Diet, the Socialist and Communist members could affect other pieces of legislation that the LDP hoped to pass, thereby forcing a compromise. In addition, the two parties could also try to block any initiative that was subject to a vote in the House of Councillors (the Upper House) because the LDP had lost its majority in 1989 and was forced to rely on support from opposition parties. Finally, the Socialists and Communists could appeal to the public, which still harboured suspicions toward the military, and thereby remind the LDP of how unpopular its pro-military policies were.

In between the LDP and the Socialists were a number of smaller opposition parties, including the Komeito (Clean Government Party) and the Democratic Socialist Party (DSP). The former was considered the political arm of a prominent religious organization known as the Soka Gakkai (Value Creation Society) and was badly divided on the issue of SDF participation in UN peace operations. The Komeito's rank and file were mostly pacifists and therefore suspicious of plans to send the SDF abroad, but the party leadership was pragmatic and felt that supporting an SDF role in peace operations would help to build bridges to the LDP. The DSP had split off from the Socialists in 1960 and had views on the SDF that were similar to those of LDP moderates.

During the period from mid-1992 to mid-1993, the LDP was able to engineer decisions to send the SDF to both Cambodia and Mozambique with little outside interference. In the case of Cambodia, LDP members were working closely with MOFA officials well before the Peace-keeping Law had been approved by the Diet. For example, Koji Kakizawa was instrumental in arranging for Cambodian leader Hun Sen to visit Japan and publicly encourage SDF participation. As a result of this and other efforts, the decision to send the SDF to UNTAC required less time than might otherwise have been expected. The decision on Mozambique, however, required intraparty negotiations owing to differences between moderates and MOFA officials. The moderates felt that Japan should concentrate on Cambodia, whereas the ministry argued that the SDF should also be sent to Africa as evidence that Japan was interested in other parts of the world besides East Asia. In the end, the ministry was able to win over the moderates with the assistance of UN Secretary-General Boutros Ghali, who made a visit to Japan when the proposal was under discussion.

In the Summer of 1993 the Japanese political system experienced a major transformation as a group of LDP members left the party, forcing then Prime Minister Miyazawa to dissolve the government and call for elections. Although the LDP made a strong showing, it did not gain a majority, and a group of eight political parties (including the JSP, the Komeito, and the DSP) managed to form a new government under Morihiro Hosokawa, and later Tsutomu Hata, that excluded the LDP. The delicate problem of how to coordinate eight disparate views was resolved by agreeing not to deviate from the policy positions of the previous LDP government. None the less, it was much more difficult for the IPCHQ to gain a consensus, because it entailed discussions with as many as eight representatives. The coalition briefly considered, but then rejected, participation in UNPROFOR and made some progress on the Golan Heights proposal before it was replaced by a new coalition in mid-1994.

At the end of June 1994, the LDP, the Social Democratic Party of Japan (SDPJ, the new name of the JSP), and another smaller party (the Sakigake) formed a new coalition and elected Tomiichi Murayama the first Socialist prime minister in nearly 50 years. At the beginning, it was unclear how two parties with extremely different views on UN peace operations would reach decisions in this area but, within weeks of taking office, Murayama announced several key policy shifts. The most significant were to drop the party's longstanding contention that the SDF was unconstitutional and to support the Peace-keeping Law. Although most SDPJ members remained opposed to expanding the military role in international security, the party was now in a position to cooperate with the LDP on sending the SDF to UN peace operations. At the same time, the LDP was less likely to take a hardline stand on dispatching the SDF overseas since a number of prominent pro-military members such as Ichiro Ozawa had left to form another party.

The LDP–SDPJ coalition took a moderate approach to participation in UN peace operations. Both parties saw the importance of sending the SDF to assist in the Rwandan refugee relief operation in eastern Zaire, especially after a request from prominent Japanese academic Sadako Ogata, who headed the UNHCR. But some coalition members later claimed that they had not known of the risks that former Rwandan government soldiers posed to SDF personnel, and accused MOFA of withholding information. The subsequent tension between the politicians and bureaucrats complicated the decision on the Golan Heights, as SDPJ members sought to ensure that the SDF would not be involved in combat in any circumstances.

During this period the main opposition party was the New Frontier Party (NFP), a union of many of the parties that had been part of the 1993–1994 governing coalition. Ichiro Ozawa and other party leaders were strongly in favour of expanding the SDF role in peace-keeping as part of a broader agenda aimed at making Japan a "normal country." Ozawa went so far as to advocate revising Article 9 of the constitution so that the government could deploy the SDF in the way that other major powers deployed their military forces. However, the new party also had elements that were opposed to such proposals, and chief among them were former members of the Komeito, with its large number of loyal supporters. The division of opinion on these issues made it very difficult for the NFP to speak with one voice.

The legislature

The National Diet, Japan's supreme law-making body, played the decisive role in the process leading to the enactment of the Peace-keeping Law in 1992. Aside from approving the law, the Diet forced the government to grant it a measure of oversight in decisions regarding the dispatch of SDF personnel to peace-keeping operations. The main concern has been a situation in which lightly armed SDF units (peace-keeping forces) are dispatched to handle combat duties such as patrolling buffer zones. Because these situations involve a higher risk of using armed force, many politicians have questioned whether the SDF can participate in them under the current interpretation of Article 9.

The need for Diet oversight in the case of peace-keeping forces emerged as a divisive issue in negotiations among the LDP, Komeito, and the DSP on the peace-keeping bill in mid-1991. Members of the DSP had argued that prior Diet approval was necessary to ensure that Japanese personnel would not be placed in high-risk situations. In addition, some politicians pointed out that Article 76 of the constitution, which requires Diet approval for dispatching the SDF for national defence, should be extended to cover proposals to send the SDF to UN peace operations. But the LDP claimed that other safeguards, notably the five conditions, were adequate and that Diet approval would simply delay sending Japanese personnel abroad.

The draft peace-keeping bill presented to the Diet in September 1991 had no provision for a Diet role in the decision-making process. The government was merely obliged to submit a report concerning Japanese participation in UN peace operations. Although the DSP agreed with the bill in general terms, it continued to insist that Diet approval was necessary. Eventually, after months of wrangling, the LDP agreed to this condition and the bill was so revised, but by this time the issue had become moot, because a proposal to freeze the dispatch of peace-keeping forces had already been incorporated in the bill. Because of the freeze, lightly armed SDF units could not be sent to undertake high-risk duties. Until the freeze is lifted, the Diet will have no direct role in the decision-making process.

The DSP also asked that the Diet be requested to approve SDF participation in UN peace operations that included duties that could be considered integrally related to infantry duties, such as transporting weapons and ammunition. Although the LDP agreed in principle that operations involving such duties should be submitted to the Diet for prior approval, no provision was included in the Peace-keeping Law. During discussions on the proposal to send the SDF to the Golan Heights, some SDPJ members argued that Japanese personnel might become involved in transporting personnel and ammunition, but there was never any discussion of submitting the proposal to a vote in the Diet.

Policy coordination with NGOs

Japanese NGO participation in UN peace operations has been on the rise over the past several years and, according to the Japanese Non-Governmental Organizations Center for International Cooperation (JANIC) in Tokyo, many Japanese NGOs now operate abroad and others intend to do so. As mentioned in chapter 7, NGOs have taken part in UN peace operations but, thus far, their activities have been self-initiated and not closely coordinated with Japanese government policy. Given the limitations on sending the SDF abroad and the relatively small size of MOFA, however, it would not be surprising if the government relies more heavily on NGOs as an alternative way to contribute to humanitarian relief operations. A good example was Somalia, where the IPCHQ found that it could not send the SDF but eventually did make a contribution to a Japanese NGO that was providing medical assistance to refugees.

It will not be a simple matter for the government to incorporate NGOs into its policy on UN peace operations, even though many organizations will no doubt welcome financial assistance. Although MOFA now has an office to oversee NGO affairs, it is not clear whether ministry officials are prepared to cooperate with NGO representatives who may have very different views on international affairs. In addition, some NGOs prefer not to have ties to MOFA or the IPCHQ, because they wish to avoid the possibility of being co-opted by the government.

Note

1. It has sent also sent civilians to monitor elections in Angola, Cambodia, Mozambique, El Salvador, and elsewhere, but these decisions will not concern us here.

PART II

4

LEGAL FRAMEWORK

Japan's active participation in UN peace operations dates from 1992, the year in which the Diet passed the Law Concerning Cooperation for United Nations Peace-keeping Operations and Other Operations (hereafter referred to as the Peace-keeping Law). Although this law has established a broad legal framework governing Japan's participation in these operations, important details have not yet been worked out and the scope of future participation remains to be settled. Resolutions of these and other issues greatly depends on domestic political developments, as discussed in the previous chapters.

This chapter describes the constitutional provisions, laws, ordinances, and jurisprudence relating to Japan's participation in peace operations. Some attention will also be devoted to the implementation of the Peace-keeping Law in recent peace operations. Subsections cover the general constitutional framework relevant to Japan's participation in, or cooperation with, UN peace operations, the legal conditions for Japanese participation in UN peace-keeping operations, and the legal conditions for Japanese participation in humanitarian assistance operations, both in natural disasters and in armed conflicts.

The constitutional framework

UN and international law in the Japanese legal system

The supremacy of the constitution

Article 98, paragraph 1, of Japan's constitution provides that the constitution shall be "the supreme law of the nation." No law, ordinance, and other act of government contrary to its provisions will have legal force or validity. Therefore, Japan's participation in peace operations must always conform to the requirements of the constitution. Although paragraph 2 mandates the Japanese government to observe international obligations stipulated in treaties and "established laws of nations" or customary international law, it is generally understood that, within the Japanese legal order, the constitution prevails over international law.[1]

The domestic legal force of international law[2]

Treaties and customary rules require no further legislative action in order to have legal force in Japan's domestic legal system. Thus, the UN Charter in its entirety has the force of law in Japan, assuming its provisions do not violate the Japanese constitution. Unlike the United States, with its UN Participation Act, Japan has no legislation generally authorizing or conditioning Japanese participation in UN activities. It is generally held that treaties and customary international law prevail over domestic statutory laws and other governmental acts.[3] Therefore, only constitutional provisions may legally restrict the Japanese government from discharging international obligations deriving from the UN Charter, treaties, and customary international law. In practice, however, Japan makes every effort to ensure that its domestic laws conform to international obligations before they become binding.

The domestic legal force of UN Security Council binding resolutions[4]

Although the constitution speaks only of "treaties" and "established laws of nations," binding resolutions adopted by the UN Security Council also appear to have the force of law in Japan. Evidence for this view is Japan's adherence to UN resolutions calling for economic sanctions against Southern Rhodesia, South

Africa, and Iraq. Respect for binding resolutions derives from two sources – the UN Charter, on which these resolutions have been adopted, and Article 98, paragraph 2, of the Japanese constitution, which requires the Japanese government to observe all international laws irrespective of their source. So understood, UN binding resolutions that conform to the provisions of the constitution will prevail over conflicting statutory provisions.

Implementation of economic sanctions resolutions [5]

In practice, binding resolutions have been implemented by applying existing laws, amending or promulgating new laws, and through cabinet and ministerial orders. Cabinet and ministerial orders must not be enacted only on the basis of a treaty or resolution (Article 73(6) of the constitution), but must implement existing statutory laws or the constitution. The Foreign Trade and Foreign Exchange Control Law provides the domestic legal basis for economic sanctions, such as those imposed on Iraq by UN Security Council Resolution 661.[6] The Immigration Control and Refugee Recognition Act provides the domestic legal basis for those UN resolutions mandating restrictions on persons crossing international borders. When the United Nations was debating whether to impose sanctions on North Korea owing to its non-compliance with the International Atomic Energy Agency's safeguards in 1994, for example, Japan considered prohibiting North Korean officials from entering Japan by applying the Immigration Act.[7]

UN Security Council resolutions that mandate or authorize military or military-related measures are especially controversial in Japan, given the possibility of a conflict with Article 9 of the constitution. This problem is discussed below.

Government branches responsible for peace operations

The cabinet and foreign relations

The cabinet is the executive organ of the state, and shall "manage foreign affairs" and "conclude treaties" (Article 73(2) and (3) of the constitution). This provision has been interpreted to mean that the power to manage foreign affairs is a plenary and exclusive prerogative of the executive. Therefore, the decision to participate in, or to cooperate with, UN peace operations is made by the executive, but must conform with the laws promulgated by the Diet (Article 73(1) of the constitution). As long as Japan's involvement in peace operations is within the constitution and legislative statutes, decisions on the timing, substance, conditions, and termination of Japanese participation in peace operations are made at the discretion of the cabinet, with one important exception.

The Diet and foreign relations

A review of the legal provisions concerning the Diet's role in foreign relations reveals a number of limitations. Although the Diet has the power to approve treaties (Article 73(3) of the constitution) for example, this power does not extend to executive agreements. Usually, specific arrangements regarding the introduction of Japanese personnel and equipment in peace operations are made orally or by exchange of notes (executive agreements) with the host country. In addition, the Diet's power of the purse (Articles 83 and 85 of the constitution) is limited because it is the cabinet that prepares the budget (Article 86 of the constitution). Moreover, the Diet customarily approves or rejects the entire budget; it rarely focuses on specific spending provisions.

The Diet does have certain prerogatives that allow it to influence foreign policy, however. Regarding the conduct of foreign affairs by the executive, the Diet may formulate the principles and rules to be observed and the organizations to be utilized (Article 66, paragraph 1, of the constitution). As "the sole lawmaking organ of the State" (Article 41 of the constitution), the Diet has passed the following laws related to Japanese participation in UN peace operations: (1) the SDF Law of 1954, which regulates the use of the SDF in peace operations; (2) the Disaster Relief Law of 1987, which regulates participation in, or cooperation with, disaster relief operations abroad; and (3) the Peace-keeping Law of 1992, which regulates participation in, or cooperation with, UN peace-keeping operations and humanitarian assistance operations in conflicts.

Diet control over participation in UN peace-keeping operations

An important exception to the executive's discretion over SDF participation in peace operations is found in Article 6, paragraphs 7–12, of the Peace-keeping Law.[8] The Diet not only discusses plans for SDF participation in UN peace operations before dispatch (Article 7 of the Peace-keeping Law),[9] it can also reject the dispatch of SDF units intended to carry out certain military tasks.[10] The

Diet considers five basic principles (discussed below) when deciding whether to approve dispatch of the SDF, but it is not precluded from taking into account other considerations it deems appropriate. The Diet, therefore, has complete discretion regarding SDF participation in certain peace operations. The same applies when the cabinet plans to extend SDF participation in those operations beyond two years.

During the debate over the peace-keeping bill, some politicians were concerned that certain political parties in the Diet might try to delay approval for participation in peace operations. As a result, the final draft of the bill included a provision (paragraph 8) that each house of the Diet endeavour to make a decision within seven working days. If the Diet is in session, therefore, a decision should be reached within 14 days, not including time in recess. If the Diet is not in session or the House of Representatives has been dissolved, a subsequent approval after the SDF dispatch may suffice (paragraph 7). Diet approval requires a simple majority in both houses. When the decisions of the two houses are different, the decision of the House of Representatives will prevail if a two-thirds majority is obtained on the second vote (Article 59 of the constitution).

The "peace provision" of the constitution and the Self-Defense Forces Law [11]

The key provision of the constitution regarding Japan's military involvement in peace operations is Article 9, which states:

> Aspiring sincerely to an international peace based on justice and order, the Japanese people forever renounce war as a sovereign right of the nation and the threat or use of force as means of settling international disputes.
>
> In order to accomplish the aim of the preceding paragraph, land, sea, and air forces, as well as other war potential, will never be maintained. The right of belligerency of the state will not be recognized.

Discrepancy between the UN Charter and the Japanese constitution? [12]

Article 2, paragraph 5, of the UN Charter stipulates that member states "shall give the United Nations every assistance in any action it takes in accordance with the present Charter." Chapter VII of the Charter stipulates various measures, including military enforcement measures, which the Security Council may take.

In Japan, potential conflict between these Charter provisions and the constitution was noted, and its consequences debated, even before admission to the United Nations in 1956. However, participation in military enforcement measures under Article 42 of the Charter is obligatory only after a member state has reached agreement to place its forces at the disposal of the Security Council in accordance with Article 43.[13] To date, no member has ever concluded such an agreement; the Security Council has been able to undertake military enforcement measures only when it has convinced a sufficient number of member states to participate. Since Japan is under no obligation to participate in such military measures, there is no discrepancy between the Charter and the constitution at present.

The constitutionality of the SDF

The prohibition of military forces found in Article 9 calls into question the very existence of the SDF. This issue has been much debated since the SDF was formed in 1954. The Japanese government interprets Article 9 as not denying Japan the right to defend itself or the right to maintain a minimum force necessary to exercise that right. Over the past 20 years, the issue of whether or not the SDF is constitutional has lost much of its political relevance as opposition parties have grown to accept the need for armed forces.

The unconstitutionality of exercising collective self-defence

Although the government believes that the SDF is constitutional, it has recognized limits on how it can be deployed. The government has consistently maintained that Article 9 bars the SDF from joining the armed forces of other nations in the exercise of the right of collective self-defence. It argues that Article 9 permits the exercise of self-defence only to the extent necessary to defend Japanese territory. Accordingly, Article 3, paragraph 1, of the SDF Law stipulates that the SDF's main task is to protect Japan from direct and indirect aggression.

Deploying the SDF abroad

In 1954, just after the SDF Law was adopted, the House of Councillors passed a non-binding resolution that prohibited the SDF from being dispatched abroad. The Japanese government has interpreted the phrase "dispatch abroad" to mean sending troops overseas with the intent of exercising the right of belligerency. Based on this interpretation, the SDF can be sent abroad to participate in duties that do not involve the use or threat of force. Article 100 of the SDF Law stipulates specific tasks that the SDF may carry out beyond Japan's borders: (1) cooperation in transportation and other functions for scientific research in Antarctica (Article 100-4), (2) air transportation for the prime minister and other national dignitaries (100-5),[14] (3) participation in relief activities abroad in accordance with the Disaster Relief Law (100-6), (4) participation in UN peace-keeping operations and humanitarian operations abroad in accordance with the Peace-keeping Law (100-7), and (5) transportation of nationals and foreigners in need of protection due to emergencies abroad (100-8).[15]

In addition, Article 99 permits the SDF to remove and dispose of explosive and dangerous materials from the sea. This article provided the legal basis for the dispatch of SDF minesweepers to the Persian Gulf in 1991 in order to dispose of mines laid by Iraq following its invasion of Kuwait. The government justified this action by arguing: (1) Article 99 does not define the geographical area of "the sea"; therefore, the SDF may carry out activities in international waters as well as in Japan's territorial waters; and (2) a formal cease-fire was in effect so that the use of force was not required in connection with disposing of the abandoned mines. None the less, the government's interpretation of Article 99 was criticized by opposition political parties and others. With the passage of the Peace-keeping Law, which permits such activities within the context of UN peace-keeping operations, it is unlikely that Article 99 will serve as the legal basis for dispatch of the SDF in the future.

The unconstitutionality of the use or threat of force abroad by the SDF

When considering the constitutionality of SDF participation in, or cooperation with, UN peace operations abroad, the key question is whether SDF duties will involve the use or threat of force. The Japanese government does not make a legal distinction between the use of force exercised within the context of a UN collective security arrangement and the use of force unilaterally exercised by Japan. According to the government, the constitution prohibits any use of force abroad. The term "the use of force" is defined in a general way as any belligerent action by Japan using material and human institutions in the context of an international armed conflict.[16] The precise meaning and scope of the phrase have yet to be clarified, however.[17]

In 1994, at the height of the tensions resulting from North Korea's alleged efforts to develop nuclear weapons, the Japanese government examined the possibility of enacting a new law that would allow the SDF to participate in, or cooperate with, the imposition of economic sanctions by the Security Council using "such measures commensurate to the specific circumstances as may be necessary."[18] This would have involved halting and inspecting ships both entering and departing from North Korean ports. Direct SDF involvement in such measures would have raised sensitive constitutional questions concerning the "use of force" beyond Japanese territory. Even SDF logistical support for those nations involved in carrying out such measures could also be regarded as constituting a "threat or use of force" under the government's current interpretation of Article 9.[19] At present, no law permits the SDF to engage in such military activities.

UN peace-enforcement operations in which Japan cannot participate

Under the government's interpretation of the constitution, Japan is prohibited from participating in any UN peace-enforcement operations that involve the use or threat of force. But again, because the term "use of force" is not clearly defined, a number of issues remain for future clarification.

Judging from the Diet debate on the Peace-keeping Law, it is fairly clear that Japan cannot participate in operations that are outside of the UN command but authorized by the Security Council under Chapter VII of the Charter to use "all necessary means." Examples of UN-authorized enforcement operations are numerous: the multinational coalition force in the Persian Gulf, the Unified Task Force (UNITAF) in Somalia, the French-led force in the Rwandan civil war, the American-led force in the Haitian situation, and a multinational implementation force (IFOR) in Bosnia–Hercegovina.

Japan is also unlikely to participate in an operation under the command of the United Nations with a mandate that "confer[s] authority for appropriate action, including enforcement action as necessary"[20] to achieve certain objectives. The UN Operation in Somalia (UNOSOM) II, established in March 1993, is the prime example of this type, and the Rapid Reaction Force deployed in Bosnia–

Hercegovina as a part of the UN Protection Force in the former Yugoslavia was also authorized to use force. Peace-enforcement actions were virtually unknown when the Peace-keeping Law was under discussion in 1991 and 1992. Prime Minister Kaifu did state, however, that Japan could not participate in UN operations such as the one in the Congo (ONUC), which was authorized to use force.[21] Based on this statement and the government's interpretation of the constitution, Japan would be prohibited from participating in this kind of UN operation.

Another question is whether or not the SDF, while remaining outside the command structure, could provide logistical and/or medical support to contingents participating in the two types of operation mentioned above. Detached from the command structure, Japan can avoid direct association with an operation authorized to use force. This rationale was utilized when the Japanese government introduced the UN Peace Cooperation Bill in 1990.[22] In Diet testimony, the Director of the Cabinet Legal Affairs Bureau argued that it would be unconstitutional for the SDF to *participate* in coalition forces that were authorized to use force. However, it would be permissible under the constitution for the SDF to *cooperate* with those forces while remaining outside the command structure. This interpretation gained little support among the opposition parties or the public, and the bill was defeated after brief deliberation. Consequently, there is little likelihood that the SDF will be allowed to provide logistical support for UN contingents authorized to use force.

A final question is whether or not the SDF can participate in a peace operation in which a multinational coalition force or a rapid reaction force is simultaneously deployed in the same area.[23] Such a situation arose in Somalia, where the traditional peace-keeping operation UNOSOM I carried out its activities under the protection of UNITAF, which was authorized to use force. Since the two operations were independent of one another, Japan could have participated in UNOSOM I because it did not involve the use of force. But the close working relationship between UNOSOM I and UNITAF would invalidate such a formalistic argument.

The discussion here has focused on the constitutionality of SDF's participation in, and cooperation with, various types of UN peace operations. However, the SDF may be dispatched outside of Japan's territory only when it is sanctioned by statutory laws. Even when constitutional questions have been settled, the SDF can undertake only those duties expressly stipulated in the SDF Law. As noted above, the most important statutory legislation is the Peace-keeping Law, to which we now turn our attention.

Japanese participation in UN peace-keeping operations

The main objective of the Peace-keeping Law was to enable the SDF to participate in military operations abroad. A small number of Japanese government officials participated in UN operations abroad prior to enactment of the Peace-keeping Law, but they could not undertake military duties.[24] Japanese military involvement in UN peace-keeping operations became possible only after the Peace-keeping Law went into effect in August 1992 (see Annex II).

Structure and scheme of Japanese participation [25]

Purpose

The stated purpose of the Peace-keeping Law is to "enable Japan to actively contribute to efforts for international peace centering upon the United Nations" through cooperation in UN peace-keeping operations and in humanitarian relief operations (Article I). It should be noted that Japan may participate in any humanitarian relief operation, whether the United Nations is involved or not, whereas Japan can join peace-keeping operations only when they are established by the Security Council or the General Assembly and under UN control.

Fundamental principle

The fundamental principle of the Peace-keeping Law is that the activities Japan carries out "shall not be tantamount to the threat or use of force" (Article II, paragraph 2). In order to realize this principle in practice, the law strictly circumscribes the UN peace-keeping operations in which the SDF may participate, so that Japan will avoid accusations that it uses force. In addition, the law defines the specific "tasks" that Japanese personnel, and particularly SDF members, may carry out. As mentioned above, the Japanese government does not support the view that UN peace-keeping operations, by definition, do not involve the threat or use of force. It must ensure that force will not be used in each peace operation in which Japan participates and each specific task that Japanese personnel undertake.

UN peace-keeping operations in which Japan may participate

Article III(1) of the Peace-keeping Law defines UN peace-keeping operations as those: (1) conducted under the control of the United Nations; (2) established by resolutions of the UN Security Council or UN General Assembly; (3) implemented by two or more participating states at the request of the UN Secretary-General and by the United Nations; (4-1) carried out impartially; (4-2) carried out only when a cease-fire agreement has been reached; and (4-3) for which consent has been obtained to carry out the operation from the host countries as well as the parties to the armed conflict, or (4-1,2,3) obtained from the host countries alone, where there have not been conflicts (in the case of preventive deployment before an actual conflict occurs). Conditions (4-1) to (4-3) are a part of the five principles discussed below.

Specific tasks Japan may undertake

The Peace-keeping Law has a unique provision that enumerates 16 specific tasks that Japan may carry out in UN peace-keeping operations (Article III(3)).[26] These tasks are called International Peace Cooperation Assignments (IPCAs). It is important here to distinguish the first six IPCAs – (a)–(f) – from the remaining IPCAs. The first six IPCAs require advanced military capabilities, and are reserved for SDF units or individual SDF personnel to carry out (Article XII, paragraph 1). When these IPCAs are carried out by SDF units, which the government refers to as peace-keeping forces,[27] Diet approval is required.[28] Owing to the "freeze" on peace-keeping forces, however, the government cannot assign these tasks to SDF units until the Diet approves separate legislation (Additional Provisions, Article II). It should be noted that the freeze does not apply to individual SDF personnel carrying out duties (a)–(f). In Cambodia, for example, eight SDF members monitored the cease-fire, patrolled buffer zones, and inspected weapons, tasks that could not be assigned to SDF units.

Because of the freeze on peace-keeping forces, distinguishing between tasks that can and cannot be carried out by SDF units is critical, though the distinction is often ambiguous. For example, if SDF units engaged in road repairs were to find a land mine, would they be allowed to dispose of it? Although minesweeping is among the frozen tasks, Cabinet Councillor Nomura Kazunari indicated that SDF units may dispose of mines in such situations.[29] On the other hand, some political leaders argue that tasks "integral" to performing tasks frozen under the law should be disallowed. This view is the likely basis for restrictions imposed on SDF transportation units sent to the Golan Heights in early 1996. The governing coalition agreed that the SDF would not be allowed to transport either ammunition or armed personnel from other contingents involved in monitoring the cease-fire. By transporting personnel or ammunition, the SDF risked becoming "integrated" in monitoring the cease-fire and patrolling the buffer zone, tasks that had been frozen.[30]

The decision to specify SDF tasks in peace operations was a deliberate one. The task of disarming people, for example, was carefully excluded from the list, so that the SDF is allowed only to collect and dispose of "abandoned weapons." Obviously, the reason for the exclusion was to prohibit the SDF from carrying out duties that involve a greater risk of using weapons. The same consideration led to the exclusion of providing military protection or escort for UN and other personnel and supplies. SDF units are also barred from conducting patrols under the freeze provision. However, there have been several cases in which the specific tasks enumerated in the law did not correspond to the situation faced by Japanese personnel in the field.

During the nationwide election in Cambodia, for example, some SDF members called on polling places, ostensibly to provide food and other supplies to UNTAC personnel, including Japanese election monitors. Some opposition parties argued that this was tantamount to patrolling a conflict area and protecting UN personnel, duties frozen or prohibited under the Peace-keeping Law. The Japanese government claimed that these SDF members were merely transporting food and supplies, a task that was acceptable under the law.[31]

Japan also sent 75 policemen to UNTAC's Civilian Police component. Their duties were to be limited to advising and supervising the local Cambodian police (Article III(3)(h)). As domestic unrest increased, however, the UNTAC commander conferred on the Civilian Police the authority to arrest people, a task not mentioned in the Peace-keeping Law. In addition, as the national election neared, the commander decided to station Civilian Police at party election offices and ordered them to escort VIPs, duties that involved protection. Concerned about possible violations of the Peace-keeping Law, the Japanese government informed UNTAC Headquarters that Japanese policemen should not be assigned to carry out these tasks.[32]

In Mozambique, Japan sent five SDF officers to the general and regional headquarters of ONUMOZ. They assisted in formulating the operation's medium- and long-term assignments and strategies. This marked the first time that SDF personnel were officially attached to the headquarters of a UN peace-keeping operation and involved in the planning of the overall operation.[33] According to the Japanese government's Implementation Plan for this operation, the five officers were allowed to carry out "formulation" of strategies concerning IPCAs specified in (a)–(p) of Article III(3). In other words, the legal basis for this function was all tasks enumerated in that article, though "formulation" of strategies for the overall UN operation itself was not specified in the law.[34]

The Peace-keeping Law does permit some flexibility in order to cope with the exigencies that may occur in the field. Article III(3)(q) of the law allows the government, specifically the cabinet, to add "other tasks assimilated to those mentioned." This provision was first invoked in Cambodia. According to the original Implementation Plan, the SDF was dispatched to carry out road construction. During its stay, however, the SDF received requests from UNTAC to undertake additional tasks, such as water purification and supplying food and accommodation to UNTAC personnel. The cabinet approved these tasks, arguing that all of them could be assimilated to the task of "transportation, storage or reserve, ... or the installation, inspection or repair of machines and apparatus" as stated in Article III(3)(p).[35]

Cooperation in kind

The Peace-keeping Law also provides for cooperation in kind (Article III(4)). Japan may provide supplies to the United Nations, UN agencies, and countries carrying out UN peace-keeping operations or humanitarian relief operations. These materials can be supplied free of charge or at below-market prices. This provision is a statutory exception to the Finance Law, which prohibits alienation of national property to others without proper compensation. Three (two in the case of humanitarian relief operations) preconditions – a cease-fire agreement, consent, and impartiality – apply in cooperation in kind (but see the recent revision, note 59). In the case of the Rwandan refugees, the Japanese government

could not provide supplies to the UNHCR for humanitarian relief operations in
Rwanda itself because no cease-fire agreement had been signed. However, it was
able to provide supplies for relief operations in neighbouring countries, where no
armed conflicts were in progress.[36]

Organization

The Peace-keeping Law establishes an International Peace Cooperation Headquarters (IPCHQ) within the Prime Minister's Office. The headquarters is under
the direction of the prime minister (chief of headquarters) (Article IV, paragraph
1; Article V, paragraph 1) and its secretariat consists of staff drawn from various
ministries, with the largest numbers coming from the Ministry of Foreign Affairs
and the Defence Agency. For each UN operation, the headquarters must prepare
a draft implementation plan and operating procedures (Article IV, paragraphs
2(1) and (2)).

An International Peace Cooperation Corps carries out the IPCAs. The corps is
composed of civil servants, individual SDF personnel, and others employed by
the headquarters (Article XI, paragraph 1). The establishment and size of the
corps are determined by Cabinet Order on each occasion that Japan decides to
participate in UN operations (Article V, paragraph 8, and Article XIX). The
corps is under the direction and supervision of the prime minister (Article XII,
paragraph 5). SDF units, although institutionally separate from the corps, can
also carry out IPCAs (Article IX, paragraph 4), but these remain under the
direction and supervision of the Director-General of the Defence Agency (Article
IX, paragraph 4, and Article XIII, paragraph 2).[37] The overall number of corps
personnel (including SDF units) may not exceed 2,000 at any one time (Article
XVIII).

The legal status of the corps and SDF personnel undertaking UN peace-
keeping operations is determined by international law derived from UN practices. The details of those practices are codified in the model agreement prepared
by the UN secretariat.[38] Before Japanese personnel are dispatched, the government confirms with the United Nations that they will be given the status referred
to in the model agreement.[39] The safety of Japanese personnel participating in
UN peace-keeping operations will be ensured by the Convention on the Safety of
United Nations and Associated Personnel adopted in December 1994.[40]

A draft implementation plan, prepared by the headquarters, specifies the

IPCAs to be undertaken, the country where IPCAs are to be carried out and their duration, the size and composition of the corps, and the equipment it will use. The same details must be specified separately when SDF units and/or the vessels and aircraft of the Maritime Safety Agency are to carry out IPCAs (Article VI, paragraph 2). The cabinet must approve the draft implementation plan (Article VI, paragraph 1), and report its approval to the Diet (Article VII). Any revision of the plan must follow the same procedure (Article VI, paragraph 13, and Article VII).

In Cambodia, an SDF engineering unit was originally dispatched to repair and construct roads and bridges. On several occasions, however, the unit was directed by the UNTAC commander to carry out tasks not specifically mentioned in the original Implementation Plan. For example, the commander requested the unit to provide medical care for UN personnel, to transport UN supplies, and to provide water and fuel for other UN contingents.[41] For each of these requests, the unit went through the lengthy process of contacting headquarters, which informed the prime minister, who then sought a cabinet decision in order to revise the plan. The Implementation Plan for Cambodia was amended three times within a year.

The Operating Procedures, prepared and revised by the chief of headquarters, contain more detailed and confidential directions to Japanese personnel in the field. They are not subject to cabinet approval, but must be prepared and revised in accordance with the Implementation Plan (Article VIII, paragraph 1) as well as the commands of the UN Secretary-General or those representing him (Article VIII, paragraph 2). Operating Procedures specify the geographical areas in the host country where the IPCAs are to be carried out, the duration and scope of IPCAs for each area, the means to implement IPCAs, including matters relating to personnel and equipment, the relationship with the relevant authorities of the host country, and suspension of IPCAs in the event of hostilities.

The Operating Procedures have been revised several times owing to exigencies in Cambodia and other operations. However, the exact number of revisions and their precise content have not been made public, except for one instance in Cambodia. There, the specific area in which SDF personnel could carry out their tasks was originally limited to the region south of Phnom Penh. But when UNTAC decided to relocate some infantry units, its commander directed the SDF unit to expand the area of its activities to include the region north of Phnom

Penh. The prime minister decided to revise the procedures in accordance with UN directions.[42]

The Peace-keeping Law, however, provides that the prime minister may delegate part of his powers to prepare and revise the Operating Procedures to a designated member of the corps in the field (Article VIII, paragraph 3). This allows the corps to respond quickly and efficiently to UN commands. In Cambodia, for example, Japanese personnel other than those in SDF units were given the authority to revise the procedures in accordance with UN commands. SDF unit personnel, on the other hand, must report to the headquarters in Tokyo when UN commands necessitate the revision of procedures. In any case, the scope of the revision must not overstep the Implementation Plan or the provisions of the Peace-keeping Law.

Command structure

The Peace-keeping Law contains numerous and potentially contradictory provisions concerning the command and control of Japanese personnel in UN peacekeeping operations. For example, it states that peace-keeping operations are to be conducted "under the control of the United Nations" (Article III(1)) and the Operating Procedures are to be prepared and revised to "conform with commands of the UN Secretary-General" (Article VIII, paragraph 2). The prime minister of Japan, however, has the power to "direct and supervise" the headquarters personnel (Article V, paragraph 2). The corps personnel, in carrying out the IPCAs, are "under the direction and supervision of the Chief" of the headquarters (Article XII, paragraph 5). SDF units are under the direction and supervision of the Director-General of the Defence Agency.

The Japanese government has explained that personnel contributed by each country are under the "command" of the United Nations. This command, or what is sometimes termed "operational control," refers to authority over the organization, deployment, conduct, and direction of these personnel. It does not include the authority to take disciplinary action, however. According to the government's interpretation of the Peace-keeping Law, operational control and the authority to take disciplinary measures rest with the government of Japan.[43] Although the government is legally obliged to ensure that its Operating Procedures conform to UN commands (Article VIII, paragraph 2), these commands must be filtered through the procedures, the preparation of which is the exclusive right of the Japanese government, before UN commands are obeyed. In this sense, operational control over Japanese personnel rests with Japan.

There is, however, an important exception to the government's obligation to conform to the UN commands when preparing and revising the Operating Procedures. The Operating Procedures specify that IPCAs are to be suspended when one or more of the three conditions – a cease-fire agreement, the consent of the parties for deployment, and impartiality – cease to exist. According to Article VIII, paragraph 2, the prime minister's decision regarding the suspension of IPCAs is not to be influenced by the command of the UN Secretary-General or his representative. Japan may disregard those commands that would lead Japanese personnel to use force for reasons other than self-defence, which would be a violation of the constitution.

The "five principles" of Japanese participation

The Peace-keeping Law established five principles that govern Japanese involvement in UN peace-keeping efforts.[44] Three of the principles are actually preconditions for Japanese participation, while the other two apply during Japan's involvement. These preconditions and requirements ensure that corps or SDF participation in UN operations will not violate the constitution. As noted above, before the corps or SDF can be dispatched, there must be a cease-fire agreement, consent of the conflicting parties, and impartiality on the part of the United Nations. IPCAs must be suspended or terminated if one of these conditions ceases to exist. In addition, once Japanese personnel have joined the operation, they can use their weapons only for legitimate self-defence.

(1)   Cease-fire

Article III of the Peace-keeping Law requires that the parties to a conflict agree to, and maintain, a cease-fire. This requirement is intended to reduce the chances that Japanese personnel would face situations in which they would need to use their weapons. The government initially interpreted Article III as requiring a *de facto* as well as a *de jure* cease-fire before Japan could participate.

In Cambodia, domestic stability deteriorated as one of the parties to the Paris Peace Agreement began to defy UN authority. The situation grew worse after the SDF contingent was dispatched in October 1992. There were a number of cease-fire violations and some direct attacks on UN personnel. In May 1993, a Japanese civil policeman was killed and several others injured. Following this tragedy, strong voices were heard in the Diet and among the public arguing that the cease-fire agreement had collapsed and demanding that Japanese personnel be withdrawn. The government refused to do this, pointing out that the defiant party was still committed to the cease-fire.[45] Since Cambodia, the government has required only a *de jure* "overall cease-fire."[46]

(2)   C o n s e n t

Under the Peace-keeping Law, Japan may dispatch its personnel only upon the consent of both the host state and other parties to the conflict (Article III(1)). They must consent not only to the UN operation itself, but also to Japanese participation in the operation and to the specific IPCAs Japanese personnel will undertake (Article VI, paragraph 1). In fact, the United Nations secures such consent, and sends a letter to Japan informing it that the parties concerned have consented to Japanese participation. Japan considers this letter as the authoritative evidence for the required consent.[47]

The Japanese position on the degree or genuineness of consent required is not clear. Some officials have expressed the view that Japan may participate in the UN Iraq–Kuwait Observation Mission (UNIKOM).[48] Iraq's consent for this operation is superficial if not forced. This view is intriguing because it does not necessarily bar Japanese participation in UN peace-keeping operations within a Chapter VII framework. But this is not the government's official position. According to UN practice, consent, especially from conflicting parties other than the host country, is a matter of degree. The United Nations has not required consent from all the parties involved in a particular conflict, such as small factions and bandits.[49] In cases in which the government of a country has disintegrated, the United Nations has no way to obtain consent for the deployment of a UN peace-keeping operation. It is not clear whether Japan can participate under such conditions.

The Peace-keeping Law allows Japanese participation in preventive deployments, which are UN operations designed to prevent conflicts from occurring. Consent for such operations will be required only from the host country. Since preventive deployments are, in theory, undertaken prior to the onset of a conflict, there is no need for either a cease-fire or impartiality toward conflicting parties. In reality, however, the areas in which preventive deployments are undertaken are usually on the verge of open conflict. Consider the situation in and around the Republic of Macedonia, for example. There, peace has been tenuous at best and the potential for armed conflict is considerable.[50]

(3)   I m p a r t i a l i t y

Article III(1) of the Peace-keeping Law requires the United Nations to be impartial in any operation in which Japan participates. Although all UN peace-keeping operations meet this requirement in theory, whether or not they do so in practice is debatable. Since the condition of "impartiality" may be subjective, the question of who determines whether or not an operation is impartial becomes important. It is not clear whether the Japanese government will determine whether or not this condition has been met, or will respect a determination made by the United Nations.

(4)   S e l f - d e f e n c e (u s e o f a r m s)

Article XXIV of the Peace-keeping Law provides that corps personnel and SDF units participating in IPCAs may use weapons within the limits considered necessary to protect themselves or other SDF or corps personnel "present with them on the same spot" (paragraphs 1 and 3). The use of arms may not cause harm to persons except in cases of legitimate defence and necessity as defined in Articles 36 and 37 of the Penal Code of Japan (Article XXIV, paragraph 4). Therefore, Japanese peace-keepers cannot directly protect non-Japanese UN personnel, nor can they be dispatched to other areas to protect Japanese or non-Japanese UN personnel. They can protect only Japanese personnel "present on the same spot" in self-defence. In addition, Japanese peace-keepers cannot be ordered to use arms. The judgement of when and to what extent weapons are to be used rests with the individual rather than with the individual's superior officers (but see the recent revision, note 59).

Because the use of weapons is restricted to self-defence of the individual, the government does not consider this to be an unconstitutional use of force. In other words, the use of weapons is not "institutionalized," so it cannot be characterized as the use of force as defined by the government. Furthermore, since weapons may be used only to protect Japanese corps personnel or SDF members, the government avoids any claim that they are engaged in collective self-defence, which is also unconstitutional.[51] These limitations, however, are considerably stricter than the UN policy on self-defence, which allows UN personnel to use force to protect their own lives, other UN personnel, as well as UN posts, vehicles, and other facilities, and to counteract attempts to prevent them from performing their UN duties.

Japanese personnel are prohibited from obeying UN commands regarding the use of weapons when such commands go beyond the provisions in Article XXIV of the Peace-keeping Law. This is made clear in the Operating Procedures, which specify that Japanese personnel may carry arms in accordance with UN commands, but omit reference to UN commands regarding the use of weapons. With respect to the use of weapons, the Operating Procedures refer only to Article XXIV of the Peace-keeping Law. In Cambodia and Mozambique, however, Japanese personnel never actually used their weapons.

Japanese corps personnel may carry "small arms" (Article XXII and Article XXIV, paragraphs 1 and 2), with the specific types of weapons designated in Cabinet Ordinance No. 268 of 7 August 1992. The weapons that Japanese SDF units may carry are not restricted by this Ordinance (Article XXIV, paragraph 3). They must be stipulated in the Implementation Plan, but the only limitation is "the spirit of the provisions of Paragraph 2 of Article III" (non-use of force) and the "limits deemed necessary by the Secretary-General" (Article VI, paragraph 4).

(5) S u s p e n s i o n   a n d   t e r m i n a t i o n

Article VI, paragraph 13(1), and Article VIII, paragraph 1(6), of the Peace-keeping Law require that IPCAs be suspended or terminated when any one of the three conditions specified in Article III of the law – cease-fire, consent of the parties, and impartiality of the operation – is no longer fulfilled. The government argued that, when UN peace-keeping forces engage in the use of force, there is a danger that Japanese contingents may also do so. Even if they do not actually use force, Japanese contingents may be considered an integral part of the action involving force. The suspension and termination requirement thus ensures that corps and SDF personnel will never be part of operations using force, and that Japanese participation in UN operations will comply with Article 9 of the constitution.

The ability to suspend or terminate Japanese participation in UN operations is of such overwhelming importance to the government that a decision on the matter can be made without consideration for the commands of the UN Secretary-General. According to Article VIII, paragraph 2, the prime minister decides matters concerning suspension of IPCAs, and his decision need not conform with the commands of the Secretary-General. This proviso may present a significant practical problem because the United Nations, in the past, has ordered troops to remain in areas where major cease-fire violations were occurring.

Under standard UN practice, every state participating in UN peace-keeping operations has the right to terminate its participation. Contributing states may withdraw their troops for any reason, including domestic requirements, as long as they give reasonable notice. Once notice has been given, the United Nations strives to find replacements or relocate existing contingents. It is not clear whether the Japanese government is required to give notice under the Peace-keeping Law, however.

By incorporating these five principles within the Peace-keeping Law, the government has sought to ensure that Japanese contributions to UN peace-keeping operations are within constitutional strictures. These principles, however, may lead to conflicts with the spirit and practice of UN peace-keeping operations. Worse, they may even call into question the effectiveness and propriety of Japanese participation in such operations.

The Japanese government tries to avoid such conflicts by securing, before the dispatch of personnel, an understanding from the United Nations on the aforementioned principles. This is accomplished by sending a *note verbale* informing the United Nations that it has decided to participate in accordance with the conditions set forth in the Peace-keeping Law. The United Nations acknowledges receipt of the *note* in a letter, which the Japanese government regards as confirmation that the United Nations agreed to its conditions. Prior to the dispatch of SDF transport units to UNDOF in the Golan Heights, for example, Japan sent a *note verbale* to the United Nations, which then issued a letter acknowledging receipt of the *note*.[52]

Japanese participation in humanitarian assistance

Humanitarian relief operations in conflict situations

Humanitarian relief operations in which Japan may participate

Article III(2) of the Peace-keeping Law defines "humanitarian international relief operations" in which Japan may participate. The requirements for participation in humanitarian relief operations are less stringent than those for peace-keeping operations.[53]

Although Japan may participate only in those peace-keeping operations authorized by a resolution of the UN General Assembly or Security Council, it may join in humanitarian efforts initiated by the General Assembly, the Security Council, the Economic and Social Council, or any of the other UN organs or specialized agencies enumerated in the Peace-keeping Law (see the Appendix to the Peace-keeping Law in Annex II). The law requires only a "request," rather than a resolution, from these international organizations. Since the administrative head of a UN organization (the Secretary-General of the World Health Organization, for example) may request Japanese participation, a collective decision by an organization is not necessary in the case of humanitarian relief operations.

More significantly, whereas peace-keeping operations must be under the command and control of the United Nations, Japan can participate in humanitarian operations led by international organizations or even individual states. Thus, operations undertaken by regional organizations such as NATO or by multinational forces such as those sent to assist the Kurds in northern Iraq could be among the "humanitarian international relief operations" in which Japan can participate.

Whereas peace-keeping operations require consent, a cease-fire, and impartiality, humanitarian relief operations require only consent and a cease-fire. Moreover, consent for the operation and for Japanese IPCAs is required only from the host state, excluding other parties in conflict. Even a cease-fire is unnecessary if the host country is not itself a party to the conflict. It might be argued that by its nature a humanitarian operation is impartial and that consent from conflicting parties is redundant. Recent history suggests the opposite. For example, humanitarian assistance in Bosnia–Hercegovina was looked upon by the Serbs as aid to the Bosnian government. Persistent attacks against UN humanitarian relief personnel in Bosnia and in Somalia point up the difficulty of sustaining the argument that humanitarian missions are impartial by definition.

In the latter half of 1994, a 283-man SDF unit took part in a relief operation for Rwandan refugees in eastern Zaire. To date this has been the only humanitarian relief operation in which Japan has participated. The request for Japanese involvement came from the UNHCR, but the operation itself was not under UN command. The Japanese government took the view that, since Zaire was not itself a party to the armed conflict, the cease-fire requirement could be omitted.

Consent to dispatch the SDF was obtained, but only from Zaire. At the time, however, soldiers of the former Rwandan government had entered the refugee camps, having fled the rebel forces. This led to sporadic fighting in and around the camps and even Zairean soldiers were involved. In order to justify SDF participation, the Japanese government adopted a loose interpretation of the requirement that, if the host country is party to the armed conflict, a cease-fire be concluded.

Because the Diet has not discussed the content of Article III(2), the precise scope of humanitarian relief operations envisaged in the Peace-keeping Law is vague. But the following principles can be discerned.

Fundamental principles

A humanitarian relief operation in which Japan participates shall not be tantamount to the threat or use of force (Article II, paragraph 2). Since the law requires consent of the host state for both the operation and Japanese participation (Article III(2) and Article VI, paragraph 1(2)), Japan may not join a humanitarian intervention mission undertaken without the consent of the country. However, as already discussed, the degree and genuineness of such consent is always difficult to ascertain.

The Peace-keeping Law requires humanitarian relief operations to be "conducted in a humanitarian spirit" (Article III(2)). Owing to its ambiguity, however, this condition is not likely to function as a legal constraint on Japanese participation.

A humanitarian relief operation will be undertaken in a situation where conflicts that "are likely to endanger international peace and security" exist (Article III(2)). Based on this condition, a humanitarian relief operation stipulated in the Peace-keeping Law can be distinguished from a disaster relief operation stipulated in the Disaster Relief Law. The phrase "likely to endanger [the maintenance of] international peace and security" appears in Article 37 of the UN Charter, and the Security Council is designated to make this judgement. When a humanitarian relief operation is undertaken without the Security Council's involvement, the Japanese government has the discretionary power to make this determination. If the Peace-keeping Law is to be invoked, it is assumed that armed conflict will have occurred in the vicinity of the site where Japan is to station its personnel.

The four principles

With regard to humanitarian relief operations, the Peace-keeping Law requires that two preconditions be met for Japanese participation: first, a cease-fire among the conflicting parties (Article III(2)), and, secondly, consent for the operation and Japanese IPCAs from the host state (Article III(2) and Article VI, paragraph 1(2)). The requirements during participation are, thirdly, the use of weapons only in self-defence (Article XXIV), and, fourthly, suspension and termination of Japanese participation when one of the first two preconditions is no longer met (Article VI, paragraph 13(2), and Article VIII, paragraph 1(6)). In the Rwandan refugees operation, the Japanese government sent a *note verbale* to the UNHCR informing of its participation in accordance with the Peace-keeping Law. In return, UNHCR acknowledged the receipt of the *note*. The details for each principle are the same as those in UN peace-keeping operations.

Specific tasks that Japan may undertake

In Article III(2), the Peace-keeping Law defines the purpose of the operation in general terms. A humanitarian relief operation is intended "to rescue inhabitants and other persons who actually or are likely to suffer from conflicts" or "to make restoration out of damage caused by conflicts." The specific tasks Japanese personnel may carry out are enumerated in Article III(3). As in the case of peace-keeping operations, these tasks are called IPCAs.

The specific tasks designated humanitarian relief IPCAs are (j) to (q) of Article III(3).[54] In other words, some of the same duties undertaken as part of UN peace-keeping operations may also be carried out as part of humanitarian relief operations. Since the six tasks requiring advanced military capabilities are not included on this list, SDF units may be dispatched to carry out any of those tasks without Diet approval.

In the Rwandan refugees relief operation, the Implementation Plan designated (j) medical and sanitary measures, (k) search or rescue of affected people, (l) distribution of food and other daily necessities for affected people, (m) installation of facilities for accommodating affected people, (p) transportation, storage or reserve, communication, construction, or the installation, inspection or repair of machines and apparatus, and (q) tasks assimilated to (p) including provision of food, water, and accommodation for those other than affected people. In other words, the Japanese government listed nearly all the tasks that can be carried out under the Peace-keeping Law. Having learned from experience, the government added those assimilated tasks that had become necessary in the Cambodian peace-keeping operation. As a result, there was no need to revise the Implementation Plan.

When 30 or so Rwandan refugees attacked Japanese and other NGO personnel in one of the camps and stole their truck, the latter called for assistance from Japanese SDF units carrying out sanitary measures there. Some 20 armed SDF personnel were dispatched from their billet to pick up the civilian personnel, who were then transported via armoured vehicle to the city of Goma.[55] Although the Japanese government justified this measure as within the scope of "transportation," there was no clear mandate in the Operating Procedures for SDF personnel to assist NGO personnel outside the billet. In a different incident, when 40 or so armed soldiers fired their automatic weapons in a camp, killing and injuring a number of refugees, armed SDF personnel visited the area to gather information and transported four of the injured refugees to a hospital in Goma.[56] As was the case in Cambodia, these incidents showed how difficult it was for SDF personnel to dispense with the provision of military protection in an unstable situation.

Organization

The same organization and procedures for UN peace-keeping operations apply for humanitarian relief operations. An Implementation Plan and Operating Procedures are devised for each humanitarian relief operation. Discussion regarding the type of weapons the Japanese corps and SDF units personnel may carry is also relevant to humanitarian relief operations.

Command structure

Because a humanitarian relief operation is not under UN command, the command and control of Japanese personnel carrying out humanitarian relief IPCAs rest with Japanese government. Corps members are under the direction and supervision of the prime minister, and SDF units are under the direction and supervision of the Director-General of the Defence Agency.

In humanitarian relief operations, coordination and cooperation among UN agencies, other national contingents, and NGOs working in the area are necessary. The Peace-keeping Law does not hinder such coordination and cooperation. In the Rwandan refugees relief operation, 22 corps personnel from the IPCHQ

and other related ministries were sent to serve as liaison and coordinating officers. They made efforts to provide for the "needs in the theater by collecting the
various kinds of information needed by the [SDF] units to implement their
assignments."[57]

Emergency relief operation in disasters

The Law Concerning Dispatch of Japan Disaster Relief Teams (hereafter referred
to as the Disaster Relief Law) was adopted in 1987 and amended in 1992 to
enable SDF personnel to participate in disaster relief operations abroad (see
Annex III). Preoccupied with the 1992 Peace-keeping Law, the Diet did not
discuss in detail the important amendment made to the Disaster Relief Law.

Purpose and principles

The purpose of the law is to provide personnel for international disaster relief
activities in cases of "large-scale disasters" abroad. The law states that such
activities will be undertaken based on requests from the disaster-stricken state *or*
from international organizations. This raises the possibility that such activities
may be undertaken at the request of an international organization, without the
consent of the host state. In more than 30 cases (between 1987 and 1994) in
which Japan sent its personnel to such operations, however, all dispatches were
made at the request of the government of the host state.[58] It is therefore difficult
to interpret this law as permitting Japan to "intervene" in a foreign country
without its consent.

Even though the law does not specify the origin of "large-scale disasters,"
they are understood to include both natural and man-made disasters. Disasters
arising from armed conflicts are not included. Many of the cases in which Japan
sent relief personnel involved natural disasters such as floods, earthquakes,
typhoons, and volcanic eruptions. Some involved man-made accidents, such as
crude oil spills in the sea or the collapse of buildings. But this changed following
the Iraqi oppression of its Kurdish minority, which caused a massive outflow of
refugees to neighbouring countries. Because this tragedy occurred before the
Peace-keeping Law had come into existence, the Japanese government dispatched medical teams to refugees camps in Turkey and Iran in accordance with
the Disaster Relief Law. None of these teams included SDF personnel. The Jap-

anese government identified the risk of epidemic in these refugee camps as a potential disaster, and did not mention Iraqi oppression.

This should be considered an exception, however. Such activities can now be carried out under the Peace-keeping Law, especially when SDF personnel are to be involved. The Diet has made clear its desire to place strict limits on the dispatch of SDF abroad in conflict situations. It would be unacceptable in such situations for the government to dispatch SDF personnel on the basis of the Disaster Relief Law rather than the Peace-keeping Law.

In 1992, the Disaster Relief Law was amended to enable SDF units to participate in such activities. Needless to say, the activities they carry out shall not constitute the threat or use of force. To date, SDF personnel have never participated in activities carried out under the Disaster Relief Law. Even if they do so in the future, they are likely to be unarmed, given the purpose of the law.

Activities that Japan may undertake

Article 2 of the Disaster Relief Law permits (1) search and rescue activities, (2) medical care, including sanitary measures, and (3) other measures to mitigate the damage of the disaster and to provide rehabilitation.These activities are called international disaster relief activities (IDRAs). SDF units may also carry out IDRAs and, in addition, may transport personnel and materials necessary for IDRAs (Article 3, paragraph 2).

Organization

Even though Article 2 provides that "a Japan Disaster Relief Team" is to undertake IDRAs, such a team is simply a group of experts from relevant national and local ministries and from the private sector. The heads of each ministry may direct their personnel to engage in IDRAs (Article 4, paragraphs 1–6). The Minister for Foreign Affairs may order the Japan International Cooperation Agency to carry out IDRAs (Article 5) and it is the same minister who coordinates the activities of personnel engaged in IDRAs (Article 6, paragraph 1). "A Japan Disaster Relief Team shall carry out its activities giving all due consideration to the requests of the Government of the disaster-stricken country" (Article 6, paragraph 2).

The law does not confer special legal status or privileges on Japanese personnel carrying out IDRAs abroad. No formal agreements are concluded between Japan and the host state regarding these operations. From the information provided by the Economic Cooperation Bureau of the Ministry of Foreign Affairs, they are taken care of in ad hoc discussions with the relevant governments.

It is the urgent and non-conflictual nature of a disaster that permits the expeditious dispatch of Japanese personnel to the site. The flexibility and simplified procedures found in the Disaster Relief Law should be understood in this context. In the Rwandan refugees crisis, some critics argued that the dispatch of Japanese personnel was delayed because the Peace-keeping Law, with its many preconditions, was the legal basis for government action. Japan could have responded much faster, they claimed, if the Disaster Relief Law had been applied. This sort of argument ignores the history of these laws as well as the Diet's reasons for passing them.

Summary

Japanese participation in UN and other peace operations is legally conditioned by Article 9, the peace provision of the constitution. According to the government's interpretation, dispatching the SDF abroad for collective self-defence or any overseas military operation involving the use or threat of force is prohibited. But the precise definition of the "use of force" remains unclear. The Peace-keeping Law allows the SDF to participate in UN peace-keeping operations and international humanitarian relief operations, both of which are strictly defined in the law. More significantly, the law enumerates the specific tasks that Japanese personnel may carry out within an operation. Any change in those tasks must be effected by revision of the Implementation Plan, which requires a decision by the cabinet. There are certain tasks not mentioned in the law or that are currently "frozen."

The SDF's experiences in Cambodia, Mozambique, and Zaire have revealed some of the problems inherent in the Peace-keeping Law. To begin with, the law is not adequately responsive to the needs of SDF and other personnel in the field, and the Japanese government has had to devise strained interpretations to cope with certain exigencies. The statutory restriction on the use of weapons by Japanese personnel (i.e. only for individual self-defence) may call into question the effectiveness and propriety of Japanese participation in military operations.

Recognizing these problems, there has been some discussion within the government concerning the revision of certain provisions of the law. At the end of 1996, however, it is still uncertain whether these discussions will bear fruit. One thing is certain: although the legal framework governing Japanese participation in peace operations has been established, many critical questions concerning details of the law have yet to be settled. Decisions made by the Japanese government must be carefully scrutinized in order to ascertain the precise scope of future Japanese participation in peace operations.[59]

Notes

1. Hisashi Owada qualifies this view, arguing that "(1) The Constitution has superior force over international treaties, except for such international treaties as those relating to the very existence of the state, such as the instrument of surrender or the treaty of peace. (2) In view of the concrete phraseology [of Article 98, paragraph 2], it is accepted that there is no difference in validity between international treaties and customary international law, with a proviso that customary international law, in view of its basic nature as *jus naturale*, is part of the law of the land, including the Constitution, and has in substance the validity that can be binding over the Constitution" (Hisashi Owada, "International organizations and national law," *Proceedings of the American Society of International Law 1995*, 1995, p. 257).

2. See Yuji Iwasawa, "The relationship between international law and national law: Japanese experience," *British Year Book of International Law*, vol. 64, 1993, pp. 344–349, 371–375.

3. An executive agreement concluded by the government alone on the basis of existing domestic laws should not be given a rank higher than statutes enacted by the Diet (ibid., p. 372).

4. See ibid., pp. 378–380; Kazuya Hirobe, "Article 98 Paragraph 2 of the constitution of Japan and the domestic effects of resolutions of the United Nations Security Council," *Japanese Annual of International Law*, vol. 36, 1993, pp. 17–32.

5. See Shigeo Kawagishi, "UN economic sanctions and domestic implementation in Japan," in *Proceedings of the American Society of International Law 1995*, 1995, pp. 348–349.

6. Security Council Resolution 661 was published in the official gazette, with the notification that the Foreign Trade and Foreign Exchange Control Law (FTFECL) would apply. In order to take specific measures stipulated in the Resolution, the Japanese government amended relevant executive orders to implement the FTFECL (ibid., p. 31).

7. *Asahi Shimbun*, morning edition, 4 June 1994, p. 2.

8. See Akiho Shibata, "Japanese peacekeeping legislation and recent developments in U.N. operations," *Yale Journal of International Law*, vol. 19, 1994, pp. 324–325; Shunji Yanai, "Law Concerning Cooperation for United Nations Peace-keeping Operations and Other Operations," *Japanese Annual of International Law*, vol. 36, 1993, pp. 59–61.

9. Article 76, paragraph 1, of the SDF Law requires the approval of the Diet when the prime minister decides to mobilize the SDF to defend against armed attacks. This is another instance of Diet involvement in foreign affairs.

10. The Peace-keeping Law distinguishes between a proposal to dispatch SDF units, which the Diet can veto, and a plan to dispatch individual SDF members attached to the International Peace Cooperation Corps, which requires no Diet action. It is also necessary to distinguish the duties the SDF units are to carry out. Those requiring relatively high military capabilities, which are enumerated in Article III(3) (a)–(f), can be vetoed by the Diet (see note 26 below and Annex II).

11. See Shibata, op. cit. (note 8), pp. 311–314, 330–332.

12. See Shigeru Kozai, "Japanese participation in United Nations forces: Possibilities and limitations," *Japanese Annual of International Law*, vol. 9, 1965, pp. 11–14.

13. See Bruno Simma and Hermann Mosler, eds., *The Charter of the United Nations: A Commentary*, London: Oxford University Press, 1994, p. 130.

14. During the 1990 Persian Gulf crisis, the Japanese government attempted to dispatch SDF aircraft to the Gulf in order to transport refugees. A cabinet ordinance was enacted on the basis of Article 100-5, but was criticized as an unacceptable distortion of this provision. In the event, no SDF aircraft were sent. See Shibata, op. cit. (note 8), p. 316.

15. Article 100-8 was added in 1994. The decision to dispatch SDF aircraft requires that safety be assured, but the provision offers no clarification of the criteria for judging "safety."

16. For the government's unified view (*toitsu kenkai*) as stated by Daikichi Ishibashi, see the House of Representatives, 122nd Session of the Diet, *Minutes of the Proceedings of the Special Committee on International Peace Cooperation*, no. 3, pp. 19–20 (18 November 1991).

17. SDF units surely constitute "material and human institutions" and the use of weapons by SDF units abroad can be characterized as the prohibited use of force. But it is not clear whether the use of weapons by individual SDF members would constitute the "institutional" use of force. The phrase "international armed conflict" is also ambiguous. From the statements of government officials, the phrase includes armed conflicts between or among domestic armed parties as in civil wars, but seems to exclude domestic civil strife or disorder.

18. The phrase is from UN Security Council Resolution 665 of 25 August 1990, which called upon member states to effectuate the sanctions imposed on Iraq by halting inward and outward shipping.

19. On 15 April 1996, Japan and the United States concluded an Acquisition and Cross-Servicing Agreement (ACSA). According to this agreement, the Japanese SDF can provide logistical support, including the provision of fuel but excluding ammunition, to the United States armed forces in the following three situations: (1) joint exercises; (2) UN peace-keeping operations; and (3) international humanitarian relief operations. The agreement applies only in peacetime, thus skirting constitutional issues

such as the exercise of collective self-defence in conflict. For the full text of the agreement, see *Asahi Shimbun*, evening edition, 15 April 1996, p. 2.

20. UN Doc. S/25354 (1993), paragraph 91, as referred to in Security Council Resolution 814 of 26 March 1993, by which UNOSOM II was established.

21. The House of Representatives, 121st Session of the Diet, *Minutes of the Proceedings of the Special Committee on International Peace Cooperation*, no. 3, p. 17 (25 September 1991). Under the terms of Security Council Resolution 161 of 21 February 1961, ONUC was urged to take all appropriate measures, including the use of force in the last resort, to prevent the occurrence of civil war in the Congo.

22. See Shibata, op. cit. (note 8), pp. 314–315.

23. Ibid., pp. 314–343.

24. Japan's Ministry of Foreign Affairs may dispatch civil servants and other civilians to participate in UN peace-keeping and election monitoring without invoking the Peace-keeping Law. The legal basis is the Ministry of Foreign Affairs Establishment Law and other related laws, which allow the ministry to send national and local public servants to international organizations. In addition, Shunji Yanai cites the ministry's "broad competence regarding international cooperation" (Yanai, op. cit., note 8, p. 61). For a list of those operations in which Japan participated before the Peace-keeping Law was enacted, see Shibata, op. cit. (note 8), p. 314, n34.

25. See Shibata, op. cit. (note 8), pp. 318–322; Yanai, op. cit. (note 8), pp. 44–61; also Hisashi Owada, "A Japanese perspective on peacekeeping," in Daniel Warner, ed., *New Dimensions of Peacekeeping*, Dordrecht: Martinus Nijhoff, 1995, pp. 103–116.

26. These tasks are: (a) monitoring cease-fires, and the withdrawal and demobilization of armed forces; (b) stationing in and patrolling buffer zones; (c) weapons inspection; (d) collection, storage, and disposal of abandoned weapons; (e) assisting in the establishment of cease-fire lines; (f) assisting in the exchange of prisoners; (g) supervising and managing elections; (h) advising on police administration; (i) advising on other administrative matters; (j) providing medical services and sanitary measures; (k) undertaking search and rescue of people affected by conflicts and assisting their repatriation; (l) distributing food and other supplies to people affected by conflict; (m) installing facilities to accommodate people affected by conflict; (n) the repair and maintenance of facilities damaged by conflicts; (o) restoring the natural environment; (p) transporting, storing or reserving, communicating, constructing, or installing, inspecting or repairing machines and apparatus not already specified; and (q) other tasks assimilated to those above, as specified by Cabinet Order.

27. In the Peace-keeping Law, the term "peace-keeping forces" appears only once in Article VI, paragraph 7, which deals with the Diet's approval when the SDF units undertake specified tasks involving advanced military capabilities. In Japan, the term, often abbreviated as PKF as distinguished from PKO (peace-keeping operations), has a special meaning, referring to a UN operation in which duties requiring relatively higher military capabilities are undertaken.

28. See note 10 above and Annex II.

29. The House of Representatives, 123rd Session of the Diet, *Minutes of the Proceedings of the Special Committee on International Peace Cooperation*, no. 4, p. 4 (10 June 1992).

30. Issues confirmed by the governing coalition relating to Japan's participation in UNDOF, 25 August 1995. The legal significance of the coalition view, however, is not clear. The Implementation Plan for UNDOF does not explicitly forbid transportation of arms and ammunition. A government official explained that, as a practical matter, the SDF will not need to transport these supplies. This statement allowed the government to avoid establishing a legal precedent. The House of Councillors, 132nd Session of the Diet, *Minutes of the Proceedings of the Foreign Relations Committee*, no. 12, p. 29 (11 May 1995).

31. Results of the Implementation of Cambodian International Peace Cooperation Assignments, pp. 174–175 (a compilation of documents regarding Japanese participation in peace operations, provided from the Ministry of Foreign Affairs).

32. Ibid., p. 172.

33. In Cambodia, three SDF officers were attached to UNTAC headquarters as liaison officers. There was no specific provision in the Implementation Plan referring to this duty; the Japanese government regarded such duties as supplemental activities necessary to carry out tasks undertaken by the SDF contingent. Ibid., p. 174.

34. Implementation Plan for Mozambique International Peace Cooperation Assignments, adopted by the cabinet on 27 April 1993, p. 12 (see note 31 above).

35. Cabinet Ordinances no. 373 of 9 December 1992 and no. 167 of 6 May 1993. The Peace-keeping Law provides for the distribution of food and other daily necessities and maintenance of facilities necessary for daily life, but only for those affected by conflict. In order to make efforts on behalf of UNTAC personnel, Article III(3)(p) was more appropriate.

36. Results of the Implementation of Rwanda Refugees Relief International Peace Cooperation Assignments, p. 201 (see note 31 above). *Yomiuri Shimbun*, morning edition, 3 August 1994, p. 3.

37. Though institutionally separate from the corps, SDF personnel in units simultaneously hold the status of the corps members and, like corps members, undertake research, analysis, and assessment of IPCAs as stipulated in Article IV, paragraph 2(3). In this instance, SDF units are under the direction and supervision of the prime minister.

38. See UN Doc. A/46/185 (1991).

39. Takahiro Shinyo, ed., *Kokusai Heiwa Kyoryoku Nyumon [An Introduction to International Peace Cooperation]*, 1995, Tokyo: Yuhikaku, p. 199.

40. UN Doc. A/49/742 (1994). Japan signed and accepted the convention on 6 June 1995. The convention is currently ratified or accepted by only six states and is not yet in force (as of May 1996).

41. Results of the Implementation of Cambodian International Peace Cooperation Assignments, op. cit. (note 31), p. 174.

42. *Yomiuri Shimbun*, morning edition, 10 February 1993, p. 1.

43. Yanai, op. cit. (note 8), p. 56; also the government position paper submitted to the Diet on 27 November 1991 in the House of Representatives, 122nd Session of the Diet, *Minutes of the Proceedings of the Special Committee on International Peace Cooperation*, no. 8, p. 17 (27 November 1991).

44. See Shibata, op. cit. (note 8), pp. 325–334.

45. *Asahi Shimbun*, morning edition, 15 May 1993, p. 7 (summary of the debate on the Cambodian operation in the House of Councillors plenary meeting).

46. In fact, such a lenient view was suggested during the debate on the Peace-keeping Law (statement by Minoru Tamba, the Director of the UN Bureau, the Ministry of Foreign Affairs, the House of Councillors, 123rd Session of the Diet, *Minutes of the Proceedings of the Special Committee on International Peace Cooperation*, no. 5, pp. 27–28, 8 May 1992).

47. In the case of UNDOF, for example, Japan received a letter, dated 8 December 1995, from the United Nations informing it that consent from the governments of Syria and Israel had been secured. The cabinet adopted the Implementation Plan for UNDOF on 15 December 1995. In the case of Mozambique, Japan received a letter, dated 23 April 1993, from the United Nations informing it that the consent of the Mozambique government and of the rebel force RENAMO had been secured. The cabinet adopted the Implementation Plan for ONUMOZ on 27 April 1993.

48. Statement of Minoru Tamba, the Director of the UN Bureau, the Ministry of Foreign Affairs, the House of Representatives, 122nd Session of the Diet, *Minutes of the Proceedings of the Special Committee on International Peace Cooperation*, no. 6, p. 11 (21 November 1991), and no. 3, p. 30 (18 November 1991).

49. See Shibata, op. cit. (note 8), pp. 335–337.

50. Specific conditions for UN preventive deployment have yet to be worked out, but the UN Secretary-General suggests that consent from the host country alone may suffice. See *An Agenda for Peace*, UN Doc. S/24111 (1992), paragraph 32.

51. The government interpretation regarding the precise circumstances in which personnel are permitted to use weapons has been fluctuating, however. Following the death of a Japanese civilian policeman in Cambodia, for example, some government leaders argued that Japanese SDF members may use weapons to protect non-Japanese personnel when such personnel are in immediate danger. *Nihon Keizai Shinbun*, morning edition, 18 May 1993, p. 2.

52. In the case of UNDOF, the Japanese *note verbale*, dated 15 December 1995, states only that a transport unit consisting of 43 members will participate in accordance with the Peace-keeping Law. There is no explicit mention of the duties stipulated in the Implementation Plan or the restrictions agreed upon by the governing coalition. With respect to the agreement of the governing coalition, see note 30 above. The UN *note verbale* acknowledging receipt of the Japanese *note* is dated 18 December 1995.

53. See Shibata, op. cit. (note 8), pp. 323–324.

54. See note 26 above for details of the tasks.

55. *Nihon Keizai Shimbun*, morning edition, 4 November 1994, p. 35.
56. *Nihon Keizai Shimbun*, evening edition, 26 November 1994, p. 11.
57. *Paths to Peace: Japan's Cooperation for World Peace* (a pamphlet provided by the Secretariat of the International Peace Cooperation Headquarters), p. 16.
58. *Activities Based on the Disaster Relief Law*, as of 1 April 1995 (a document provided by the Economic Cooperation Bureau of the Ministry of Foreign Affairs, with an explanatory note).
59. On 5 June 1998, the Diet passed a bill that makes several revisions to the Peace-keeping Law. The most significant of these is a change in how Japanese personnel, including SDF members, may use weapons. Under the 1992 law, personnel were permitted to use weapons in self-defence based on their own judgement, rather than on the command of a superior officer. The revision states that, in principle, a Japanese commanding officer will issue the order to personnel to fire their weapons. The government had previously argued that, if Japanese personnel used their weapons on an individual, rather than a collective, basis, they could not be accused of using armed force, and hence were not violating the official interpretation of Article 9.

A second revision allows the government to provide equipment and supplies (i.e. "cooperation in kind") to humanitarian operations even if a cease-fire is not in effect. Previously, Japan had not been able to offer supplies to humanitarian operations unless all the conditions for sending Japanese personnel abroad had been met. This ruled out sending assistance to humanitarian operations in countries where the central government had collapsed. The final revision allows the government to send personnel to monitor elections not supervised by the United Nations. Japan is now considering whether to send personnel to monitor the Bosnia-Hercegovina national election that will be overseen by the Organization on Security and Cooperation in Europe.

On 28 April 1998, the Japanese government submitted a bill to implement the new Guidelines for US–Japan Defense Cooperation. Although this legislation deals with changes necessary to improve bilateral security cooperation, it also contains provisions that relate to Japanese participation in UN peace operations. For example, Article 7, paragraph 3, of the bill permits the SDF to inspect ships on the high seas under a UN Security Council resolution imposing economic sanctions. But, in accordance with Article 9, the SDF can only "request" ships to halt and is not permitted to force captains to comply. In addition, the bill allows the SDF to provide logistical support to US troops using force. However, the SDF can venture no further than "rear-area" support, with "rear area" defined as high seas and air space in which no belligerent actions are likely to be undertaken. Based on this precedent, the SDF should also be allowed to provide rear-area support to UN contingents engaged in peace enforcement.

5

FINANCIAL AND BUDGETARY ASPECTS

At a time when the United Nations faces enormous financial pressures, Japan has been among its most generous and conscientious members.[1] Japan is the second-largest contributor to the UN budget in absolute terms after the United States and is rarely, if ever, in arrears. Despite its recent economic difficulties in the aftermath of the "bubble economy," the Japanese government has faced no budgetary obstacles in participating in UN peace operations. Its emphasis on the non-military components of foreign policy, coupled with the relatively small size of the SDF and stringent preconditions on dispatching military personnel abroad, makes it unlikely that Japan will participate in more than one or two UN peace operations at any one time. The extremely low cost of operations in relation to the overall defense budget makes it unlikely that financial pressures will inhibit or otherwise influence Japanese policy.

Budget disbursements for UN peace operations

Despite efforts to establish a unified peace-keeping budget, the United Nations continues to assess member states separately for individual peace-keeping operations.[2] In Japan, these assessments are covered by funds disbursed from the Ministry of Foreign Affairs (MOFA). Table 5.1 lists contributions during the

Table 5.1 **Ministry of Foreign Affairs annual contributions to the UN peace-keeping budget**

	1990	1991	1992	1993	1994
US$ million	26.8	88.4	247.9	357.2	484.1
¥ billion	3.6	11.4	30.7	37.3	46.7

Table 5.2 **International Peace Cooperation Headquarters disbursements (¥ million)**

Operation	1992	1993	1994
Cambodia (UNTAC)	690	740	–
Mozambique (ONUMOZ)	–	230	300
Zaire	–	–	200
Golan Heights (UNDOF)	–	–	–
Total	690	970	500

period 1990–1994. The rapid rise in Japan's disbursements is an accurate reflection both of the government's heightened interest in peace-keeping operations as well as of the increasing global demand for such operations in the post–Cold War period. In comparison with other member countries, Japan's contributions in 1996 accounted for more than 15 per cent of the total peace-keeping budget, second to the United States (31 per cent) but ahead of Germany (9 per cent) and France (8 per cent). MOFA also handles contributions for humanitarian relief activities that are overseen by the UNHCR, and is currently among the largest contributors to this agency.

The government also allocates funds to the International Peace Cooperation Headquarters (IPCHQ) and Defence Agency to cover participation in UN peace operations. Funding for the IPCHQ is dispensed from national budget reserves (*yobi-hi*) based on individual cabinet decisions (see table 5.2). The headquarters must cover the costs of stationing its officials at host-country embassies, sending SDF officers to peace-keeping training centres, and other related expenses. The Defence Agency, on the other hand, uses funds from its annual budget allocation. The agency pays the costs of transporting personnel and equipment to the host country. SDF members sent on UN peace missions receive their regular salaries

Table 5.3   **Defence Agency disbursements (¥ billion)**

Operation	1992	1993	1994	1995	1996
Cambodia (UNTAC)	7.5	2.9	–	–	–
Mozambique (ONUMOZ)	–	1.0	0.7	–	–
Zaire	–	–	5.7	–	–
Golan Heights (UNDOF)	–	–	–	–	
Total	7.5	3.9	6.4	–	
Total defence budget	4,551	4,640	4,683	4,723	4,845

and a special peace-keeping allowance. The agency also provides supplemental insurance coverage.

Total Defence Agency expenditures for participation in peace-keeping operations are given in table 5.3. Funding for SDF participation in ongoing peace operations, or those that are imminent, is included in the agency's annual budget request to the Ministry of Finance in August. Funds for the second year of operations in Cambodia, Mozambique, and the Golan Heights were dealt with in this manner. If, on the other hand, a new peace operation is undertaken in the course of the fiscal year (1 April to 31 March), funds are transferred from other Defence Agency accounts. As with other countries participating in peace-keeping operations, expenses incurred by the Defence Agency are eventually reimbursed by the United Nations.[3] But because these reimbursements are based on the average cost for providing soldiers among all participating countries, they rarely cover the total expenses incurred by advanced industrial nations such as Japan. No reimbursements are made for official participation in humanitarian missions overseen by the UNHCR, such as the 1994 Rwandan refugee relief operation in Zaire.

It should be emphasized that Japan's large financial contributions to the UN peace-keeping budget and UN-directed humanitarian missions contrast with its modest outlays for direct participation in UN peace operations. As noted, Japan has only recently begun sending personnel to peace-keeping operations, and the scope of its participation remains heavily constrained by a host of domestic and international factors. Consequently, Defence Agency expenditures on UN peace operations to date have represented only a small fraction of Japan's overall defence spending (see table 5.3).

Notes

1. For a discussion of the United Nations' financial problems, see the 1993 report of the Independent Advisory Group on UN Financing, *Financing an Effective United Nations*, Ford Foundation.

2. Assessments are usually made every six months. Exceptions are the two peace-keeping operations funded through the regular UN budget (UNTSO in the Middle East and UNGOMAP in Kashmir) and one funded by voluntary contributions (UNFICYP in Cyprus).

3. In the case of UNDOF, the IPCHQ requested that Japan be allowed to send a contingent larger than the Canadian one it replaced. The United Nations agreed but indicated that it would not reimburse the IPCHQ for the additional personnel.

PART III

6

MILITARY CAPABILITIES

In this chapter, the military capabilities of Japan's military branch, the Self-Defence Forces (SDF), are discussed. Established in 1954, the SDF is primarily concerned with defending Japanese territory from external attack. In this mission it is assisted by the United States, with which it has close ties through the US–Japan Mutual Security Treaty. Under the provisions of this treaty, US armed forces have been stationed in Japan continuously since the end of the Occupation in 1952. The United States has also pledged to use its nuclear weapons to defend Japan, which was one factor behind the Japanese government's decision to renounce possession of such weapons. Despite US protection, the Japanese government has had a consistent policy of steadily increasing the capabilities of the SDF.[1] Although one of the smallest military forces in East Asia in terms of manpower, it is among the most potent in terms of its conventional defence capabilities.

The SDF has had a troubled history. Within Japan, many believe that the armed forces were responsible for the devastation and suffering Japan experienced during and after World War II. When it was decided to re-establish a military in the early 1950s, the government took steps to institute a system of civilian control that would ensure only a minor policy-making role for the armed forces. The SDF was placed under the control of the Defence Agency, composed of civilian bureaucrats. The Defence Agency, in turn, was not a full-fledged ministry but an agency located in the Prime Minister's Office. In an effort to avoid employing officials with ties to the pre-war military institution, the agency was staffed by personnel transferred from other ministries. Today it continues to be influenced by the Ministry of Foreign Affairs (MOFA), the Ministry of Finance, and the Ministry of International Trade and Industry, whose personnel are seconded to important positions within the agency.

Although most Japanese have come to accept the need for adequate defence against attack, few are in favour of having the SDF go abroad with the intention of using military force. In addition, East Asian countries such as China and South Korea, which suffered depredations at the hands of the Japanese Imperial Army, have been especially critical of efforts to expand the SDF role beyond defence. Thus, despite pressure from the United States to take a greater role in regional security, Japan has been reluctant to do so. According to the government inter-pretation of Article 9 (for details, see chap. 4), the SDF is permitted to use force only in connection with defending Japan. The SDF may not, for example, co-operate with US forces in combat operations outside Japanese territory, nor may it take part in UN collective security actions that involve the use of force.

The Japanese government has also had enormous difficulty securing the right to dispatch the SDF to UN peace operations that do not involve the use of force. In light of what had happened in the 1930s, the political climate in Japan remained acutely sensitive to any changes that could be interpreted as loosening restrictions on the military. When the SDF was established by law in 1954, there was strong opposition to incorporating any duties that would involve sending it abroad. But a dilemma arose two years later when Japan became a member of the United Nations: namely, should it begin sending troops to UN operations? MOFA believed that, at the very least, the government could dispatch SDF per-sonnel to military observer groups or other operations that did not involve the use of force, yet was unable to gain sufficient domestic political support for its view.

The idea that the SDF could be part of Japan's contribution to international security was not seriously debated until the end of the Cold War, after Japan had been severely criticized during the Persian Gulf crisis. Even so, few Japanese advocated changes that would allow the SDF to take part in combat operations. The majority eventually came to support a modest revision of the SDF law that would permit the government to dispatch the SDF to traditional UN peace-keeping operations and other situations where the risk of conflict was minimal. Yet even this modest revision was opposed by progressive political parties, backed by a significant segment of public opinion. As a result, over a year of negotiations and Diet debate was required before the peace-keeping bill became law in 1992. Under this law, the SDF has been sent to three UN peace-keeping missions and one UN-coordinated humanitarian relief operation, which are discussed at greater length below.

General force structure

The Japanese military is divided into three services: Ground, Maritime, and Air Self-Defence Forces (henceforth, the GSDF, MSDF, and ASDF, respectively). Although these three services rank well behind other East Asian countries in terms of manpower, with about 240,000 personnel, the SDF is equipped with some of the most modern weapons systems available by virtue of its large defence budget and its close ties to the United States. To cite just a few examples, the MSDF has *Aegis*-class destroyers, the ASDF has some 175 F-15s as well as AWACs aircraft, and the GSDF has deployed the *Patriot* missile defence system. Moreover, the SDF participates in a wide range of joint military exercises with US armed forces, particularly the US Navy, which has exposed the SDF to advanced military strategy and tactics. Japanese armed forces must be regarded as among the most potent in East Asia.

None the less, the Japanese military has both limitations and serious inadequacies. Constitutional constraints on using military force abroad prevent the SDF from possessing weapons systems that are considered purely offensive. In addition to its well-known policy of never acquiring, manufacturing, or using nuclear weapons, the government has also prohibited the acquisition of certain conventional weapons systems with force-projection capabilities. Throughout the post–World War II period, all weapons systems have been justified as necessary for what the Japanese government terms "defensive defence" *(senshu boei)*, a strategic doctrine that limits SDF duties solely to the defence of Japanese territory. But the criteria used to determine whether a weapon is defensive or not are often ambiguous. For example, a long-running debate pits the Defence Agency against certain opposition parties over the need for in-flight refuelling capabilities. The former argues that air tankers are necessary so that aircraft can provide continuous defence of Japanese territory in the event of an air attack. The latter contend that acquiring such capabilities would be unduly provocative to neighbouring countries. As a consequence of these concerns, the SDF has no air tankers, bombers, or fixed-wing aircraft carriers. It also has comparatively few air transports and landing craft, which has had an impact on the SDF's ability to engage in UN peace operations abroad.

Among the other deficiencies that have affected Japan's participation in UN peace operations are out-of-date and formalistic training practices, a pronounced lack of integration among the three services, generally poor logistics, and less than adequate command and control capabilities. These problems are attributable in a general way to the absence of an imminent threat to Japan and the policy prohibiting the SDF's dispatch abroad. With the passage of the Peace-keeping Law and participation in UN peace operations, however, the government has begun to scrutinize certain of these limitations and to consider ways to rectify them.

The three services have varying capabilities. The MSDF, which is responsible for patrolling Japan's extensive maritime boundaries and critical sea lanes, is considered the premier branch of the Japanese armed forces. Prior to passage of the Peace-keeping Law, it was involved in minesweeping operations in the Persian Gulf following the defeat of Iraq by UN-authorized forces. In UN peace operations, the MSDF has been largely confined to transport duties. But, given conditions in the South China Sea and the Taiwan Straits and on the Korean peninsula, the possibility remains that the United Nations might consider maritime operations such as monitoring a cease-fire in the Spratly Islands or enforcing economic sanctions against North Korea. The MSDF has held joint training exercises with the US Navy, including simulated maritime interdiction, but such duties involve the use of force. Whether they could be justified under the current interpretation of the constitution is, at best, uncertain. Much would depend on the extent of the crisis and the degree of US pressure on Japan.

The ASDF is also highly regarded, especially its air defence capabilities, but it too plays only a supporting role in UN peace operations. The main duty has been transport of personnel and equipment to and from the operations in which the GSDF has participated. As will be discussed below, the service has had some difficulty handling the large amount of equipment required in these operations.

Owing to constitutional restraints, the ASDF is not prepared to send fighter aircraft to participate in peace-enforcement duties such as those undertaken by NATO in the former Yugoslavia.

The GSDF has been given less attention than the other two services in recent years, owing to the waning of the Cold War. Although it is the largest of the three services in terms of personnel, the ground forces faced an uncertain period with the demise of the Soviet Union. The Soviet forces stationed on islands at the extreme southern end of the Kurile chain (referred to as the *Hoppo Ryodo* or Northern Territories) were at one time regarded as a direct threat to northern Japan. The removal of these troops combined with the general decline of the Russian military has reduced the importance of the GSDF mission.

The passage of the Peace-keeping Law brought new opportunities, however. Although the maritime and air services have played key support roles, it is the ground forces that have the training necessary to handle many of the main peace-keeping duties: road construction and repair in Cambodia, movement control in Mozambique, medical and sanitation duties in Zaire, transportation in the Golan Heights (for details, see below). As noted in the previous chapter, lightly armed GSDF units (referred to as peace-keeping forces) are prevented from engaging in certain activities that might involve the use of force, including patrolling buffer zones and supervising disarmament of belligerent parties.

On 28 November 1995, the Japanese government approved a new National Defence Programme Outline, replacing the 1976 version. The new outline envisages increased participation in future UN peace operations and contains several items that bear directly on the SDF's ability to participate in them. Regarding basic military capabilities, the outline indicates that the SDF will be restructured "in both scale and function" in order to be able to respond to "a variety of situations," among them international peace cooperation and disaster-relief activities. This restructuring includes measures to improve intelligence-gathering, command and control, as well as logistical support capabilities.

Japan has sought to use the close working relationship between the SDF and US military forces as the basis for expanding its participation in UN peace operations. In May 1994 it was reported that a bilateral working group was considering specific ways by which the two armed forces could assist each other in such operations. As a result of these efforts, the Acquisition and

Cross-Servicing Agreement signed by the two countries in April 1996 made specific reference to UN peace operations, allowing the SDF and US forces to supply fuel, spare parts, and other logistical assistance as necessary.

Specialized capabilities for peace operations

Because the SDF has only recently begun to participate in UN peace operations, it has had no time to develop specialized capabilities. Given the constraints imposed by the Peace-keeping Law, moreover, the Japanese government can dispatch the SDF only to traditional UN peace operations, and it cannot send SDF units to handle infantry duties until the freeze on dispatching peace-keeping forces is lifted. So, for the time being, the SDF will have little choice but to focus on the type of non-military support duties such as construction and sanitation that it has undertaken in previous peace operations. Below is a description of the duties the SDF has carried out in past peace operations, and those it is currently carrying out in the Golan Heights.

UNTAC (September 1992 – September 1993)

The majority of the 683 personnel sent to the UN Transitional Authority in Cambodia (UNTAC) were members of a GSDF engineering battalion assigned to repair roads and bridges in Takeo Province. During their stay, the engineers repaired 80 kilometres of road and fixed 40 bridges. At the request of UNTAC and with the permission of the Japanese government, the contingent also provided food, lodging, and medical care to UN personnel, and supplied water and fuel to other UN units. In the weeks before the election, the SDF provided logistical support for the elections and agreed to supply polling places with food, water, and other necessities. A group of eight GSDF members was also assigned to monitor the cease-fire and supervise disarmament. This duty posed the most risk to SDF personnel in Cambodia: one officer assigned to investigate cease-fire violations was regularly fired upon. The MSDF transported most of the personnel and heavy equipment for the operation from Japan to the port of Sihanoukville and also brought in food and drinking water from Thailand and Singapore. The ASDF also transported personnel and equipment from Japan to the air base at Pochentong near Phnom Penh. These flights were made via air bases in both Thailand and the Philippines.

ONUMOZ (May 1993 – January 1995)

A 53-man contingent of GSDF, ASDF, and MSDF personnel was sent to handle what the United Nations refers to as "Movement Control" (MOVECON), which involves various administrative duties necessary to transport supplies efficiently. The length of the mission meant that the 5 staff officers rotated once and the 48 MOVECON personnel were rotated twice, so that a total of 154 took part in the assignment. The contingent was split into two groups, with one located in the city of Matola and the other in the city of Dondo (later moved to Beira). Each group handled the arrival of UN personnel and supervised the off-loading of, and arranged for customs clearance for, supplies at airports near these cities. In addition, the contingents coordinated transportation of supplies to warehouses and to the various UN contingents involved in the operation. The five SDF officers were assigned to ONUMOZ headquarters to serve as liaisons.[2]

Zaire (September–December 1994)

At the request of the UN High Commissioner for Refugees (UNHCR), some 280 SDF personnel were sent to handle medical, sanitation, and water purification duties in refugee camps near the city of Goma in eastern Zaire. The medical team consisted of personnel from all three services. Between October and December 1994, the team handled more than 2,000 patients, most suffering from cholera, dysentery, and malaria. The sanitation unit focused on efforts to prevent the spread of malaria, while the water purification unit ensured that refugees had a regular supply of potable water. In addition, the ASDF played a critical role in the operation by transporting supplies from an air base in Kenya to Goma.[3]

UNDOF (February 1996 –)

The UN Disengagement Observer Force (UNDOF) logistics unit has been sent 45 GSDF personnel, replacing one portion of the Canadian peace-keeping contingent. The primary task is to transport supplies to the Austrian and Polish infantry units that man observation posts and patrol the Golan Heights buffer zone between Israel and Syria. According to the SDF Implementation Plan, 43 GSDF members were also expected to oversee storehouses, keep roads in repair, and maintain mechanical equipment. The Japanese contingent is stationed at Camp Ziouani on territory occupied by Israel. Two SDF officers have been assigned to UNDOF headquarters at Camp Faouar to act as liaisons. The SDF contingent is expected to remain in the Golan Heights for at least two years, rotating every six months. Japan's International Peace Cooperation Headquarters (IPCHQ) also dispatched 63 ASDF personnel in order to provide logistical support for the transportation unit when it first arrived in the Middle East. The ASDF continues to provide supplies and to transport GSDF to and from the region.[4]

Logistics and technical aspects

In two of the three peace operations in which the SDF has participated, the primary function has been duties related to the transportation of personnel and supplies. In Mozambique, the SDF contingent was attached to Movement Control (MOVECON), the unit that handled customs clearance and coordinated transportation of UN personnel and supplies to locations throughout the country. This involved mainly administrative tasks. By all accounts, SDF personnel performed ably and were cited by the United Nations for superior service.

The Golan Heights mission was very different from those previously undertaken by the SDF, however. In the Golan Heights, the SDF was assigned to replace a Canadian unit that had been handling the transportation of personnel and supplies to units that patrolled the buffer zone. This raised concerns among Japanese officials that, in an emergency, the SDF might be called upon to transport arms, ammunition, and armed peace-keepers preparing to defend the UN mission. Some Japanese political leaders argued that the SDF risked becoming involved in monitoring the cease-fire, a duty currently frozen under the Peace-keeping Law. In order to avoid this situation, the IPCHQ sought UN assurances that the SDF contingent would not be asked to transport personnel or supplies in support of actions involving military force, as defined by the Japanese government.

As with most military organizations, the SDF has made every effort to send self-sufficient units to UN peace operations. Self-sufficiency means inclusion of personnel to handle financial, police, personnel, and administrative matters for the unit. The alternative is to work out arrangements in which Japanese personnel are integrated with other peace-keeping units, which may involve a host of complications arising from different languages and customs. To date, the SDF has sent self-sufficient contingents in most cases. In Cambodia, the SDF had little choice: Japanese personnel were not sent until six months after UNTAC had begun operations and, because housing was no longer available, the SDF spent its first weeks constructing a temporary encampment. Of the 600 SDF members sent, nearly 200 were assigned to support those carrying out engineering duties The SDF also set up a camp near one of the refugee camps in Zaire, where there was no suitable housing. The UNHCR preferred to have self-sufficient units such as the SDF because it made coordination of the operation much simpler. The 45-man contingent sent to the Golan Heights is also self-sufficient, although it will be part of a Canadian logistics unit. Mozambique has been the only operation in which Japan sent SDF personnel who were not fully independent, having relied on Portuguese and Italian units for food, water, and electricity.

Stand-by/rapid reaction arrangements

One of the major difficulties facing the United Nations has been the need to reduce the length of time between a decision by the Security Council to set up a peace-keeping operation and the arrival of personnel and equipment. Given the often tenuous circumstances during this period, it is imperative that peace-keepers establish their mission as rapidly as possible. But, in the absence of a standing force, the United Nations is forced to negotiate with individual countries, most of which have no personnel or equipment dedicated to UN peace-keeping.

As an important step toward alleviating this problem, the General Assembly passed a resolution in December 1993 calling for the establishment of a UN Stand-by Arrangements System (UNSAS). The main aim of this system is to provide the United Nations with a database of military units and equipment available from member countries for UN peace-keeping and the amount of time needed to respond to a UN request. To date, 60 countries have pledged to provide the United Nations with some 80,000 personnel, including headquarters support, communications, construction, logistics, air services, health services, and civilian police.[5] Although the Japanese government supports the existence of such a system, domestic concerns have made participation difficult. The idea that certain units would be earmarked for use in peace operations has raised concerns that this arrangement represents an unconditional commitment to the United

Nations. Some have argued that such a commitment is an infringement of Japan's Peace-keeping Law, which requires that certain preconditions be met before a decision is reached. Japan has therefore refrained from listing units or equipment in the database.

In a related development, the governments of Canada, the Netherlands, and Denmark have been pursuing efforts to establish a permanent UN rapidly deployable mission headquarters. Based in the United Nations office in New York City, a staff of 15–20 military officers would be available for dispatch to areas in which peace operations were contemplated. These officers could then provide accurate information on which to base operational planning. Once again, the Japanese government supports the proposal but there is little likelihood that SDF officers will participate. Under current Japanese law, SDF officers can be sent abroad for only a limited range of duties, such as serving as military attachés or for training purposes.[6]

UN peace-keeping procedures

Under the Peace-keeping Law, the cabinet must first approve SDF participation in any operation, as well as the Implementation Plan that outlines the duties the SDF is to carry out. During the decision-making process, the government dispatches one or more fact-finding teams to the host country. At least one SDF officer is included on the team so that a military perspective informs the decision to participate and the scope of duties to be undertaken. Once participation has been approved, the prime minister orders the SDF to begin its preparations.

Although the Japanese government makes every effort to support UN peace operations in which the SDF takes part, it is also concerned to avoid any infringements of the Peace-keeping Law. One way to ensure that those directing the peace-keeping operations are aware of the constraints on the SDF is by placing Japanese staff in operations headquarters. This was not possible in the case of Cambodia, because the SDF arrived some six months after UNTAC had begun functioning, or in Zaire, where the UNHCR coordinated but did not direct humanitarian assistance efforts. But Japanese personnel were attached to ONU-MOZ headquarters in Mozambique and have been sent to UNDOF headquarters in the Golan Heights.

Under the current Peace-keeping Law, SDF and UN standard operating procedures differ in important respects. One of the most critical of these differences concerns the use of weapons. The UN view on the use of military force has expanded in the past 40 years. At first, UN peace-keepers were permitted to fire their weapons in strict self-defence, which included actions to protect the lives of other peace-keepers. Since the 1970s, however, this definition has been revised to include "defence of mission," which allows peace-keepers to use force against those who try to impede or prevent UN duties from being carried out.[7] SDF members, in contrast, are not permitted to use their weapons in defence of the mission, nor is it clear whether they can do so to protect other UN personnel. The possibility that, having come under attack, SDF personnel might not assist their fellow peace-keepers is a potential source of friction in future operations.

The Japanese government has also been concerned about the weapons carried by SDF personnel. In both Cambodia and Mozambique, they were permitted to have side-arms (9 mm) and automatic rifles (7.62 mm). In these operations, the government judged that the SDF faced minimal risks and required only light weapons. Moreover, in Cambodia the SDF engineers were operating in the vicinity of a French infantry unit, while in Mozambique the MOVECON companies were located near ONUMOZ headquarters. In Zaire, on the other hand, the SDF faced a riskier situation: the refugee camps were known to harbour soldiers of the former Rwandan government, which raised the possibility of armed clashes with the Rwandan Patriotic Front. To ensure that the SDF contingent could defend itself in the event of hostilities, the SDF requested that it be permitted to take two mounted machine guns. Although peace-keepers from other nations routinely carry a variety of heavy weapons, including machine guns and mortars, this request led to a political debate within the Japanese government. One side was adamantly opposed to equipping the SDF with machine guns because, under the Peace-keeping Law, the contingent was to be withdrawn if there was any sign of instability, while the other side felt that SDF personnel should have adequate means to protect themselves. In the end, a compromise was reached and the SDF was allowed to take a single machine gun mounted on an armoured vehicle. The same debate arose prior to the dispatch of peace-keepers to the Golan Heights. In this case a request for three machine guns was reduced to two.

The Japanese government has also made clear its intention to retain command and control over SDF personnel. Specifically, Japan has asserted its right to withdraw personnel in the event of armed conflict. Although other countries have exercised the right to withdraw their contingents, Japan is among the few to make explicit its right to do so. As noted elsewhere, the government is very concerned that SDF personnel should not be placed in situations in which they would be forced to use their weapons. With the death of a Japanese police officer in Cambodia in Spring 1993, the government came under pressure to effect a withdrawal because one party to the conflict, the Khmer Rouge, appeared to be on the verge of unilaterally ending the cease-fire. But MOFA officials and LDP politicians expressed great concern about the possible ramifications for the UN operation if Japan withdrew, not to mention the international criticism that would be directed at the Japanese government. In the end, Japanese personnel remained in Cambodia. None the less, it is not difficult to imagine future circumstances in which the government once again would come under this sort of domestic pressure.

Force-projection and lift capabilities

As indicated above, the SDF is prohibited from using force abroad and therefore has limited force-projection and lift capabilities. Specifically, the air-lift capabilities of the ASDF and the sea-lift capabilities of the MSDF have been developed for the purpose of defending Japan, not for transporting personnel, equipment, and supplies to peace operations in distant countries. The number of air and sea transports procured by the SDF is in accordance with the National Defence Programme Outline, which was approved in 1976. According to the 1995 edition of *Defence of Japan*, the ASDF has 15 C-130H aircraft, while the MSDF has a total of 9 landing ships. Since these are necessary for the SDF to carry out its primary duty of defending Japan, only a small number can be assigned to UN peace operations.[8]

The limitations of Japan's air-lift capabilities were noted in Cambodia. Because of their limited operational range, the ASDF C-130 aircraft were forced to divide the trip into several legs, stopping in Okinawa and the Philippines en route from the ASDF base near Nagoya to Cambodia. In the case of human-itarian relief efforts in Zaire, the C-130 did not have sufficient cargo space to hold all of the equipment required by GSDF personnel. As a result, the Japanese government was forced to charter an *Antonov* air transport from Russia.[9] Once in Africa, the ASDF used three of its C-130s to transport goods from Nairobi in

Kenya to the airport at Goma. The Japanese government has considered procuring a larger transport with increased operational range, but this may incur domestic opposition because such an aircraft would have force projection capabilities.

The scale and location of UN peace operations have not caused problems for the MSDF. In the case of UNTAC, much of the heavy equipment and supplies was transported by sea to the port at Sihanoukville. The MSDF had the necessary supply and landing ships to handle this task, without compromising its ability to defend Japan. If equipment and supplies need to be unloaded away from modern port facilities, however, the MSDF may not be able to provide the type of landing craft capable of handling these conditions.

Readiness and training programmes

One major obstacle for SDF personnel has been their lack of overseas experience. With the exception of some officers, most have never performed their duties anywhere but in Japan. There has been little attention to language training or environmental conditions in foreign countries. Moreover, SDF duties relate either to defending Japan or to assisting in disaster relief. Until 1992, the SDF had no experience in, or little knowledge of, UN peace-keeping operations. Following the passage of the Peace-keeping Law, however, the SDF has begun to develop an international perspective and to take measures to improve its readiness for future peace operations.

Since 1992, the Defence Agency has sent bureaucrats and uniformed officers to study peace-keeping strategies. Prior to the Cambodian operation, for example, a group of SDF officers was sent to the UN Training Centre in Sweden to receive instruction in standard UN peace-keeping procedures.[10] In addition, prior to each UN peace operation in which they have participated, SDF personnel have received special training to expose them to various contingencies they might confront. However, because SDF units are currently barred from infantry duties such as monitoring cease-fires or patrolling buffer zones, there has been no need for comprehensive training in peace-keeping techniques.

Notes

1. A major reason for the high level of SDF capabilities is a defence budget that is ranked third largest in the world (about US$47 billion in 1995). Yet it should be

noted that Japan's military expenditures are far less impressive if calculated as a percentage of gross domestic product and if the high cost of procuring weaponry is also taken into account. In letting defence contracts, the Japanese government's primary consideration has been to maintain the nation's defence industrial base. Weapons that have been indigenously developed and manufactured, or have been produced under licence from foreign manufacturers, are preferred to those purchased off-the-shelf, but this is a costly strategy. In addition, the government bars Japanese defence contractors from exporting weapons systems, which leads to short and expensive production runs. As consequence, the weapons procured by the Defence Agency are at least twice or three times more expensive than those of the United States. See Norman D. Levin, Mark Lorell, and Arthur Alexander, *The Wary Warriors: Future Directions in Japanese Security Policy*, Santa Monica, CA: Rand, 1993.

2. *Defence of Japan 1995*, Tokyo: Japan Times, pp. 101–116.

3. Ibid., pp. 106–116.

4. *Japan Times*, 3 February 1996.

5. *Progress Report of the Secretary General on Standby Arrangements for Peacekeeping*, UN Doc. S/1996/1067.

6. The law has also prevented SDF personnel from being sent to the UN Department of Peace-Keeping Operations.

7. On the development of UN policy on the use of armed force, see F. T. Liu, *United Nations Peacekeeping and the Non-use of Force*, International Peace Academy Occasional Paper Series, Boulder, CO: Lynne Rienner, 1992.

8. Masashi Nishihara has proposed having the United States air-lift SDF peace-keepers where necessary; see his "Japan-US Cooperation in UN Peace Efforts," in Selig Harrison and Masashi Nishihara, eds., *UN Peacekeeping: Japan and American Perspectives*, New York: Carnegie Endowment for International Peace, 1995, pp. 163–175.

9. Prior to sending the SDF to Zaire, the Japanese government had asked the United States to air-lift equipment. An agreement was reached, but the United States later withdrew its offer.

10. Since 1992, the SDF has sent over 10 of its members to UN peace-keeping training sessions. In 1997 a senior GSDF officer went to Malaysia for a month-long course in cease-fire surveillance.

7

CIVILIAN ASSISTANCE

This chapter covers civilian (non-military) participation in UN peace operations and includes discussions on human rights and security, election monitoring, emergency rescue services, and humanitarian relief and aid. Much of the Japanese participation in these activities can be traced to the 1970s when growing economic prosperity began to generate external pressures on Japan to play a more active role in global affairs. At the same time, a new-found sense of confidence among the Japanese, based on their economic accomplishments, created a desire to play such a role. The reduction of East – West tensions from the late 1980s provided an incentive to take part in the increasing scope of UN activities.

It was during this latter period that Japan began to send MOFA personnel to serve as election monitors and adopted the Disaster Relief Law, which allowed the government to dispatch medical and rescue teams overseas. Government efforts to contribute to UN peace operations were given a major boost with the passage of the Peace-keeping Law in 1992, which established the International Peace Cooperation Headquarters (IPCHQ) with the purpose of coordinating Japan's participation in these operations. Although much attention has been focused on the role of the SDF, the Peace-keeping Law establishes guidelines for non-military participation as well.

As previously noted, under the 1992 law the Japanese government must ensure that certain preconditions (the five principles) are satisfied before SDF personnel can be sent to UN peace operations. This is also the case for civilian personnel and cooperation in kind. In other words, according to the law, any official assistance either to peace-keeping operations or to humanitarian relief activities can be provided only if these preconditions have been met. Since the scope of official assistance is narrow, the government has advocated changes in the law that would allow greater flexibility. For instance, it has proposed that the five preconditions not be applied to the dispatch of civilians or to the provision of goods to humanitarian relief operations. But this will require a political consensus on revising the law.[1] Others have suggested that the government invoke the 1987 Disaster Relief Law, which has fewer restrictions on dispatching personnel. But this law covers natural disasters, not situations arising from armed conflict. Another option is to promote non-governmental organizations as an alternative to official assistance efforts.

Japan's first non-governmental organizations (NGOs) developed in the late 1960s. These organizations were affiliated with religious groups and focused on assistance to South-East Asian nations during the Viet Nam War. A second wave of NGOs was established in the late 1970s with the onset of the Indo-Chinese refugee crisis. Today there are some 200 Japanese NGOs, three-quarters of which aim to provide medical, financial, or technical assistance to foreign countries. But the majority have fewer than five staff members and little experience abroad. Their lack of resources and experience place them at a distinct disadvantage in competition with well-financed NGOs from North America and Europe.[2]

The government has made some effort to encourage the growth of NGOs as a way to increase and enhance Japan's contribution to global social welfare. In 1989, MOFA began offering subsidies to NGOs, providing US$1 million. By 1994, the amount had risen to US$5.4 million. In addition, both the Ministry of Posts and Telecommunications and the Environmental Protection Agency provided funding. The former set up a special postal savings account in which a percentage of the accumulated interest would be used to finance NGOs, while the latter established a fund to assist NGOs working on environmental issues. In 1993, a total of US$370 million was distributed to 31 groups for 75 projects overseas. MOFA opened the Private Assistance Support Office in 1994 to improve ties to NGOs.[3]

At the same time, there have been numerous complaints over Japanese government policy toward NGOs. Some have been concerned that the government has introduced subsidies as a way to control them. Once they come to rely on state funding, critics argue, NGOs will be forced to act in accordance with official government policy in order to continue receiving these funds and will thus risk losing their capacity for independent action. In addition, there has been criticism that strict government regulations on non-profit organizations prevent NGOs from making their activities more widely known to the Japanese public, thereby weakening their ability to attract donations. Finally, many Japanese government officials have a thinly disguised contempt for NGO staff members, regarding them as interlopers in matters that the government bureaucracy alone should handle. As a result, there is little interaction between the two sectors.[4]

The distant relationship between government and NGOs may be changing, however, as Japan seeks to play a more visible role in world affairs. Government ministries and agencies clearly do not have the funding or personnel to handle all aspects of Japan's burgeoning international ties and will need to rely on NGOs for assistance in certain areas. Japan-based NGOs that aspire to play a role in international relief activities know that government support can be a critical factor in helping them survive in competition with NGOs from Europe and North America.

Human rights monitoring and security

In connection with its decision to participate in the Cambodian peace-keeping operation, the Japanese government dispatched 75 police officers to the UN Civilian Police (CIVPOL) unit. This was not the first time that civilian police had been included in UN peace-keeping operations, but the police contingent in Cambodia was the largest ever sent. According to UNTAC guidelines, the Civilian Police were "to supervise, control, guide and coordinate activities of police forces of all the factions of Cambodia," in order to "ensure that no violation of human rights takes place."[5] Given the poor state of the Cambodian police forces, however, it was soon apparent that CIVPOL personnel would be expected to do more than oversee their Cambodian counterparts. Among the additional duties CIVPOL undertook were guarding the offices of Cambodian political parties and escorting party leaders. This placed the UN police at great risk, especially in the weeks leading up to the national election in May 1993.

The Japanese contingent, which had been recruited by the National Police Agency from prefectural police offices, faced difficult conditions. Unlike the SDF engineering battalion, which was located in a single province, Japanese policemen were assigned, in groups of 5 and 10, to local police stations throughout Cambodia, including the volatile north-west sector of the country. Initially, the Japanese government showed little concern for police assignments, perhaps assuming that CIVPOL personnel would be serving only in a super-visory capacity as the UNTAC had indicated. But the government soon received reports that some of its police officers were serving in high-risk areas and were handling duties that went beyond merely supervising Cambodian police. It sent several requests to UNTAC Headquarters warning that Japanese policemen were there only in a supervisory capacity, and asked that those in risky areas be re-assigned to other parts of Cambodia. UNTAC refused to relocate the Japanese, arguing that, if they were moved to safer locations, other contingents would demand similar treatment.

In May 1992, less than a month before the election, a group of Dutch and Japanese police officers was ambushed in the north-western section of the country. One of the Japanese policemen, Haruyuki Takata, was killed and three others wounded. Takata's death shocked the Japanese public, who had been led to believe the Cambodian operation would not involve bloodshed. At the same time, there were disturbing reports that other Japanese policemen had deserted their posts owing to concerns about personal safety. A public debate arose in Japan and some felt the Japanese contingent should be withdrawn because the cease-fire had apparently broken down. At one point, Prime Minister Miyazawa declared that he would suspend Japanese participation if conditions worsened. Although the government continued to uphold its commitment, some UN offi-cials worried about what might happen in the event the Japanese withdrew. Some predicted that the entire operation might unravel.[6]

The death of Takata and allegations that some of the Japanese civilian police had not fulfilled their duties dampened Japanese enthusiasm for participation in future UN CIVPOL operations. Although the senior National Police Agency official in charge of the contingent urged continued involvement, the Interna-tional Peace Cooperation Headquarters has not sent Japanese policemen to other peace operations since Cambodia. In 1993 the government rejected a request to send Japanese policemen to the large CIVPOL contingent in Mozambique, and in 1996 it rejected a request to send personnel to the CIVPOL contingent in Bosnia and Hercegovina.[7]

The role of the United Nations in protecting human rights is not just a matter of government policy, but has been attracting a great deal of interest and concern throughout Japanese society. Efforts to increase public awareness of human rights issues were given a boost when in 1993 the International Movement Against All Forms of Discrimination and Racism (IMADR) became the first Japan-based NGO to be accepted by the NGO committee of the UN Economic and Social Council. With the committee's sanction, the IMADR received prior notification of the Council's agenda, was able to participate in UN human rights committee hearings, UN seminars, and conferences, and was permitted to submit written opinions on various Council issues. Established in January 1988, the IMADR now has more than 27 member organizations and 132 individual members in 20 countries.[8]

The opening of the Asia-Pacific Human Rights Information Centre in December 1994 was another important step in raising public awareness of human rights issues. The centre's primary purpose is "to collect and disseminate information and conduct research on human rights issues in the region."[9] A number of individuals are also active in promoting the importance of human rights issues. One of the best known is Yozo Yokota, a professor at the International Christian University, who has served as UN Special Rapporteur for Human Rights in Myanmar.

Election monitoring

Japan began to assist UN efforts to monitor elections in the late 1980s following Prime Minister Noboru Takeshita's 1988 International Cooperation Initiative, which had called for more active Japanese participation in activities promoting peace and security. The first case in which MOFA arranged to send election monitors was Namibia, which held a national referendum in 1989. Some 30 government workers were dispatched to the UN Transition Assistance Group (UNTAG). The following year, six monitors were dispatched to ONUVEN, which covered the national election in Nicaragua. In each of these cases, MOFA asked for volunteers from the central government and placed a request with the Ministry of Local Autonomy (MLA) to recruit monitors from prefectural and city governments. Both MOFA and the MLA sent five members to the team.[10]

Under the Peace-keeping Law, the government also began to encourage NGO participation. The first election-monitoring operation under the new law was the UN Angola Verification Mission (UNAVEM II). In September 1992, Japan dispatched three civilians who had been selected from the government and one recruited from the non-governmental sector. Japan sent 15 civilians to the UN Observer Mission in El Salvador (ONUSAL), which monitored elections in El Salvador in March and April 1994. In addition, Japanese personnel participated in supervising national elections in Cambodia (1993) and Mozambique (1994). MOFA has continued to send its own personnel to observe elections that are not overseen by the United Nations, such as those in Russia (1993) and South Africa (1994).

In addition to those Japanese sent to election-monitoring duties by the government, others have participated in UN election efforts on a volunteer basis. In Cambodia, some 32 Japanese civilians were among the 730 UN volunteers who helped prepare for, and supervise, the voting process. The Japanese government agreed to send televisions and radios to assist them in this effort. In the run up to the election, one of the Japanese volunteers and his interpreter were killed in April 1993. This incident, followed just a few weeks later by the death of police officer Takata, had a demoralizing effect on Japanese public opinion. There were also reports indicating that Japanese volunteers were among those who withdrew from their assignments as tensions rose prior to the election. As in the case of its civilian policemen, however, the Japanese government contended that the volunteers were subject to far more dangerous conditions than they had expected based on information provided by UN coordinators.[11]

Emergency rescue services

The Disaster Relief Bill was submitted to the Diet and adopted in September 1987. Although the government had sent personnel abroad to assist in disaster relief, it submitted this bill to provide a clear legal basis for future participation in international relief operations (for details see chap. 4). Under the law, Disaster Relief Teams were formed, consisting of rescue, medical, and administrative units depending on the nature of the emergency. Personnel for the teams are drawn from various ministries and NGOs. At first, the 1,800-strong body included policemen, Maritime Safety Agency officers and firemen, doctors and nurses, and emergency rehabilitation workers. Since 1992, SDF personnel have been permitted to take part as well, but have yet to do so. The teams are organized by the Japan International Cooperation Agency, which is part of MOFA. Between 1987 and 1994, 32 teams were sent to 22 countries. For example, teams were sent to aid earthquake and tidal wave victims in Nicaragua in 1992, flood victims in Nepal in 1993, people trapped in the rubble of a collapsed building in Malaysia in 1993, and earthquake victims in Colombia in 1995.

The Disaster Relief Law and the Peace-keeping Law are meant to cover different types of circumstances. In general, the former allows the government to send personnel and supplies to assist in relief operations in the wake of natural and man-made disasters, whereas the latter permits the government to send military personnel to handle situations that arise from, or may involve, armed conflict. There are significant differences between the two laws in terms of the decision-making process involved and the time required to dispatch personnel. Before sending the SDF abroad, the IPCHQ must gain the approval of both politicians and bureaucrats, an effort that may entail weeks of negotiations. A Disaster Relief Team, on the other hand, can be dispatched on the orders of the Minister of Foreign Affairs within 48 hours.

Choosing to invoke the Peace-keeping Law or the Disaster Relief Law thus has important consequences. In the case of assisting the Rwandan refugees in eastern Zaire, the government chose the Peace-keeping Law because of the potential risks to Japanese personnel. But, in so doing, it was unable to respond quickly to the crisis, with cabinet approval for the operation requiring nearly a month. By the time the SDF reached the refugee camp in Goma, the worst of the disaster was over and contingents from many other countries had left. Although the SDF did provide useful medical and sanitation services, these were of a routine nature. In Japan, some observers criticized the government for not invoking the Disaster Relief Law, which would have permitted a more expeditious response.[12]

Another reason the SDF, not a Disaster Relief Team, was sent to Zaire had to do with the "service package" approach of the UN High Commissioner for Refugees (UNHCR) to coordinating relief work. Under this approach, the UNHCR asks a government to handle one or more aspects of the relief operation. To simplify logistical matters, these units are expected to be self-sufficient. Unlike the SDF, neither the Disaster Relief Teams nor most Japanese NGOs have the capability to undertake self-sufficient operations, which is another reason for their absence in many UN rescue operations.[13]

Humanitarian relief and aid

Japan's participation in UN humanitarian relief operations, as with most other forms of civilian assistance, has been handled mainly by the government. For many years, it focused on making financial contributions to international organizations such as the UNHCR and the Red Cross, both of which specialize in humanitarian relief activities. Even today, Japan provides a great deal of financial and material assistance to support such activities. Sending government workers to assist in relief work has been more problematic, especially because MOFA has far fewer personnel than the foreign ministries of advanced industrial countries. Over the past 10 years, however, the establishment of Disaster Relief Teams and the emergence of NGOs has offered new ways for Japan to play a substantive role in these relief efforts.

Among the first Japanese NGOs to become involved in humanitarian relief operations was the Association of Medical Doctors in Asia (AMDA), which was formed in 1984 by Shigeru Suganami, then a young medical student. Suganami had visited Indo-Chinese refugee camps and was frustrated that he was not permitted to assist the doctors there. After completing medical school, Suganami set up AMDA, hoping to attract doctors from throughout Asia. Today the organization has some 8,000 members from 15 Asian countries including India, Bangladesh, Nepal, and the Philippines. AMDA has sent multinational teams of physicians to more than 14 countries. Physicians from AMDA have assisted refugees in Somalia and Zaire. For his efforts, Suganami was presented with the Boutros-Ghali Award in 1995.

Several other Japanese providers of civilian medical care have also joined UN peace operations. The Japan Emergency Team, a group composed of university students and company employees, has participated in efforts to assist Kurdish, Somalian, and Bosnian refugees. The Japan Red Cross sends trained medical personnel to numerous locations, and sent two teams of nurses to refugee camps bordering Rwanda.[14] The Rwanda Campaign Committee was formed for the specific purpose of providing medical treatment for victims of the civil war in that country.[15]

The real breakthrough came in Cambodia, where Japan was involved in all aspects of the peace process. Not only did the Japanese government provide substantial funding for efforts to rebuild the country, but Japanese citizens took part as UN volunteers and donated food and medicine. In addition, a number of

Japanese NGOs also provided aid and assistance. Among the many groups participating was the Foundation for the Support of the United Nations, begun by Japanese businessmen in 1988, which opened a factory to produce prosthetic devices and has expanded its service throughout a country in which thousands of people have lost limbs as a result of land mines.[16]

In its efforts to assist Somalia, MOFA was prevented by law from sending personnel or goods. Instead, it pledged US$100 million in financial assistance and sought to sponsor Japanese NGOs as an alternative contribution. As of late 1992, however, there were no Japanese NGOs operating in Somalia to which the MOFA could offer support. Given the unstable circumstances and the risk of armed conflict, it was not hard to understand why. An AMDA representative dispatched in early 1993 decided that his organization could not risk building a clinic in Somalia. Eventually, AMDA and the Africa Education Fund sent two doctors to a Somali refugee camp in north-east Kenya in January 1993. AMDA also sent doctors to Djibouti to aid Somalian refugees there. The Japan Emergency Team sent eight of its members to Somalia for about three months to distribute medical supplies, rice, wheat, powdered milk, and other goods.[17]

The Japanese government was also unable to send the SDF to the war-torn republics of the former Yugoslavia, but it did provide some US$1.5 million in financial assistance in 1994. Japanese NGOs too have sought to aid international relief efforts. The Japan Emergency Team worked with the UN Medical Evacuation Committee to bring out victims for medical treatment, and the Association to Aid Refugees provided US$110,000 in financial assistance so that hospitals in Croatia and Bosnia could purchase medical equipment and pharmaceuticals.[18]

In the Rwandan refugee relief operation, the government provided supplies, including large tents and 30 tons of pharmaceuticals. Total official aid to the UNHCR was US$44 million, including US$9 million in emergency humanitarian assistance and US$32.3 million in financial aid. In addition, private contributions reached US$237 million. NGOs were also active in the relief effort. Some 40 Japanese civilians attached to 10 different NGOs were involved in humanitarian relief efforts. Among these was the Japan Red Cross Society, which sent a small number of doctors and nurses to Zaire and Tanzania for periods of one to six months. And, long after global concerns about Rwanda had waned, the Rwanda Campaign Committee continued to operate a clinic in eastern Zaire that served some 120 patients a day. Because of a decline in UNHCR funding, the committee was forced to use its own financial resources to remain open.[19]

It is not yet clear to what extent the SDF and Japanese NGOs have developed, or will develop, a beneficial working relationship. With its air-lift and logistics capabilities, the SDF has the potential to provide critical assistance to Japanese NGOs working in the field. In Rwanda, one AMDA representative voiced concern that the ASDF paid little attention to the needs of his and other Japanese NGOs. He pointed out that the most difficult aspect of establishing operations in a foreign country was arranging for transportation of supplies. Whereas other air forces gave priority to supplies destined for home-country NGOs, the ASDF did not. Its shipping priorities were determined by the UNHCR. In future, however, the NGO office in MOFA may be able to provide improved coordination with the SDF.[20]

Notes

1. In 1998, the Peace-keeping Law was revised to allow cooperation in kind whether or not the five preconditions have been satisfied.
2. Kenzo Moriguchi, "Nation faces greater call for efforts to aid refugees," *Japan Times*, 4 January 1995. One example of NGO competition is the effort to gain acceptance by the UN Economic and Social Council. A committee made up of members from 19 countries meets every two years to decide which groups should qualify as UN-funded NGOs.
3. "NGOs call for government backing," *Daily Yomiuri*, 9 November 1994; "The role of NGOs in Japan," *Mainichi Daily News*, 2 November 1994; Moriguchi, op. cit. (note 2).
4. Michio Katsumata, "Official aid, private aid: Finding a balance," *Nikkei Weekly*, 23 October 1995; Moriguchi, op. cit. (note 2).
5. UNTAC, Document No. 4848, "Summary of tasks to be carried out by CIVPOL in Cambodia."
6. Philip Shenon, "Is Japan ready for greater world role?" *International Herald Tribune*, 25 October 1993.
7. *Asahi Shimbun*, 14 January 1996.
8. *Daily Yomiuri*, 24 April 1993.
9. *Daily Yomiuri*, 11 September 1993.
10. Shunji Yanai of MOFA states that the ministry has the right to dispatch personnel to peace-keeping under its "broad competence regarding international cooperation." See his "Law Concerning Cooperation for United Nations Peace-keeping Operations and other Operations," in *Japanese Annual of International Law*, no. 36, 1993, p. 61, n28.

11. *Mainichi Daily News*, 10 April 1993.
12. Moriguchi, op. cit. (note 2); *Japan Times*, 4 November 1994.
13. Moriguchi, op. cit. (note 2).
14. *Japan Times*, 17 August 1994.
15. *Japan Times*, 20 July 1995.
16. *Japan Times*, 2 December 1993.
17. *Daily Yomiuri*, 28 December 1992.
18. *Nikkei Weekly*, 16 May 1994.
19. *Japan Times*, 5 August 1994; *Daily Yomiuri*, 6 August 1994.
20. *Daily Yomiuri*, 9 November 1994.

ANNEXES

Annex I

JAPANESE PARTICIPATION IN UN PEACE OPERATIONS (AS OF I JANUARY 1997)

Period	Country/zone	UN acronym	Personnel	Note
1988	Afghanistan–Pakistan border	UNGOMAP	1 MOFA official	Unarmed observer
1988	Iran–Iraq border	UNIIMOG	1 MOFA official	Unarmed observer
1989	Namibia	UNTAG	27 civilians	Election monitors
1990	Nicaragua	ONUVEN	6 civilians	Election monitors
1991	Iraq–Kuwait border	UNIKOM	1 MOFA official	Unarmed observer
1991–92	Cambodia	UNAMIC	1 MOFA official	UNTAC preparation
1992	Angola	UNAVEM II	3 civilians	Election monitors
1992–93	Cambodia	UNTAC[c]	8 SDF officers[a]	Military observers
			41 civilians	Election monitors
			75 civilian police	Police oversight
			600 SDF engineers[a]	Construction
1993–95	Mozambique	ONUMOZ[c]	5 SDF officers[a]	Liaison
			48 SDF members[b]	Transport control
			15 civilians[a]	Election monitors
1994	El Salvador	ONUSAL	15 civilians[a]	Election monitors

Period	Country/zone	UN acronym	Personnel	Note
1994	Zaire	Rwandan refugee relief operation^c	22 SDF/MOFA	Liaison
			283 SDF	Medical and sanitary
			118 SDF	Air transport
1996–	Golan Heights	UNDOF^c	2 SDF officers^a	Liaison
			43 SDF^a	Transport

a. Rotated once.

b. Rotated twice.

c. Total Japanese military personnel in foreign operations on behalf of the United Nations (1992–1996):

UNTAC	1,216
ONUMOZ	154
Rwandan refugee relief mission	423
UNDOF	90

Annex II

LAW CONCERNING COOPERATION FOR UNITED NATIONS PEACE-KEEPING OPERATIONS AND OTHER OPERATIONS, 1992

(1992 Act No. 79) (Unofficial Translation)

Chapter I: General Provisions

(Purpose)

Article I

The purpose of this Law, is, with a view to extending an appropriate and prompt cooperation for United Nations Peace-Keeping Operations and Humanitarian International Relief Operations, to set forth a framework for the implementation of International Peace Cooperation Assignments by stipulating the procedures for preparing Implementation Plans and Operating Procedures for International Peace Cooperation Assignments, the establishment of the International Peace Cooperation Corps and other matters, to take such measures as those to extend Cooperation in Kind for United Nations Peace-Keeping Operations and Humanitarian International Relief Operations, and thereby to enable Japan to actively contribute to efforts for international peace centering upon the United Nations.

(Basic Principles of Cooperation for United Nations Peace-Keeping Operations and Humanitarian International Relief Operations)

Article II

1. The Government shall cooperate effectively for United Nations Peace-Keeping Operations and Humanitarian International Relief Operations by appropriately coordinating the implementation of International Peace Cooperation Assignments, Cooperation in

Kind, cooperation extended by those other than the State related to such implementation and cooperation, and other cooperation under this Law (hereinafter jointly referred to as "the implementation of International Peace Cooperation Assignments and Others") as well as by mobilizing the creativity and expertise of the personnel engaged in the implementation of International Peace Cooperation Assignments and Others.

2.   The implementation of International Peace Cooperation Assignments and Others shall not be tantamount to the threat or use of force.

3.   The Prime Minister shall, in the implementation of International Peace Cooperation Assignments and Others, represent the Cabinet and direct and supervise the respective administrative divisions under Implementation Plans for International Peace Cooperation Assignments.

4.   To achieve the objective of Paragraph 3 above, the heads of Administrative Agencies Concerned shall cooperate with the Chief of the International Peace Cooperation Headquarters for the implementation of International Peace Cooperation Assignments and Others.

(Definitions)

Article III

For the purposes of this Law, the following terms shall have the following definitions:

(1)   "United Nations Peace-Keeping Operations" means operations that are conducted under the control of the United Nations, and upon the basis of resolutions of the General Assembly or the Security Council of the United Nations, to ensure the observance of agreement to prevent the recurrence of armed conflicts among the parties to such conflicts (hereinafter referred to as "the Parties to Armed Conflicts"), to assist in the establishment of a ruling apparatus by democratic means after the termination of armed conflicts or to maintain international peace and security in coping with disputes, provided that such operations be implemented by two or more participating countries at the request of the Secretary-General of the United Nations (hereinafter referred to as "the Secretary-General") and by the United Nations without any partiality to any of the Parties to Armed Conflicts, in cases where agreement to cease armed conflicts and maintain the cessation has been reached among the Parties to Armed Conflicts and where consent for the undertaking of such operations has been obtained from host countries as well as the Parties to Armed Conflicts, or from host countries alone unless there have occurred armed conflicts.

(2)   "Humanitarian International Relief Operations" means operations other than those implemented as United Nations Peace-Keeping Operations, that are conducted in a humanitarian spirit, and upon the basis of resolutions of the General Assembly, the Security Council or the Economic and Social Council of the United Nations or at the request of international organizations listed in Appendix, to rescue inhabitants and other persons who actually or are likely to suffer from conflicts which are likely to endanger

international peace and security (Whereas these conflicts are hereinafter referred to simply as "Conflicts", these inhabitants and persons are hereinafter jointly referred to as "Affected People".) or to make restoration out of damage caused by conflicts, provided that such operations be implemented by the United Nations or other international organizations, or the member States to the United Nations or other countries (referred to in (4) below as "the United Nations and Others"), in cases where consent for the undertaking of such operations has been obtained from host countries and, should the host countries be the Parties to Armed Conflicts, agreement to cease armed conflicts and maintain the cessation has been reached among the Parties to Armed Conflicts.

(3) "International Peace Cooperation Assignments" means all the following tasks implemented for United Nations Peace-Keeping Operations and the tasks provided for in (j) to (q) below implemented for Humanitarian International Relief Operations, wherein the incidental tasks are included respectively, provided that those tasks are conducted in Overseas Areas:

(a) monitoring the observance of cessation of armed conflicts or the implementation of relocation, withdrawal or demobilization of armed forces as agreed upon among the Parties to Armed Conflicts;

(b) stationing and patrol in buffer zones and other areas demarcated for preventing the occurrence of armed conflicts;

(c) inspection or identification of the carrying in or out of weapons and/or their parts by vehicles, other means of transportation or passersby;

(d) collection, storage or disposal of abandoned weapons and/or their parts;

(e) assistance for the designation of cease-fire lines and other assimilated boundaries by the Parties to Armed Conflicts;

(f) assistance for the exchange of prisoners-of-war among the Parties to Armed Conflicts;

(g) supervision or management of the fair execution of congressional elections, plebiscites and other elections or votings assimilated thereto;

(h) advice or guidance for and supervision of police administrative matters;

(i) advice or guidance for administrative matters not covered by (h) above;

(j) medical care including sanitary measures;

(k) search or rescue of Affected People or assistance for their repatriation;

(l) distribution of food, clothing, medical supplies and other daily necessaries to Affected People;

(m) installation of facilities or equipment to accommodate Affected People;

(n) measures for the repair or maintenance of facilities or equipment damaged by Conflicts, which are necessary for daily life of Affected People;

(o) measures for the restoration of natural environment subjected to pollution and other damage by Conflicts;

(p) transportation, storage or reserve, communication, construction, or the installation, inspection or repair of machines and apparatus, not covered by (a) to (o) above.

(q) other tasks assimilated to those mentioned in (a) to (p) above, as prescribed by Cabinet Order.

(4) "Cooperation in Kind" means the alienation, free of charge or otherwise at the price lower than the current price, of goods which are necessary for United Nations Peace-Keeping Operations or Humanitarian International Relief Operations to the United Nations and Others engaged in such operations.

(5) "Overseas Areas" means areas outside Japan, the high seas inclusive.

(6) "Receiving Countries" means foreign countries, the high seas not inclusive, where International Peace Cooperation Assignments are undertaken.

(7) "Administrative Agencies Concerned" means the administrative agencies referred to in paragraph 2 of Article 3 of the National Government Organization Law (Law No. 120 of 1948) and the special agencies referred to in Article 8-3 of the said Law, as designated by Cabinet Order.

Chapter II : International Peace Cooperation Headquarters

(Establishment and Duties)

Article IV

1. The International Peace Cooperation Headquarters (hereinafter referred to as "the Headquarters") shall be established within the Prime Minister's Office.

2. The Headquarters shall be responsible for the following duties:

(1) Preparation of the draft of implementation plans for International Peace Cooperation Assignments (hereinafter referred to as "Implementation Plans");

(2) Preparation or revision of operating procedures for International Peace Cooperation Assignments (hereinafter referred to as "Operating Procedures");

(3) Research for identifying the details of International Peace Cooperation Assignments necessary to be undertaken in receiving countries, assessment and analysis of effects of the International Peace Cooperation Assignments having been implemented, and liaison with the staff of the United Nations and other persons in receiving countries, with a view to properly making the revision referred to in (2) above;

(4) Operation of the International Peace Cooperation Corps (hereinafter referred to as "the Corps");

(5) Request for cooperation to Administrative Agencies Concerned for the implementation of International Peace Cooperation Assignments, entrusting of transportation and request for cooperation to those other than the State;

(6) Cooperation in Kind;

(7) Research concerning the implementation of International Peace Cooperation Assignments and Others, not covered by (3) above, and the dissemination of knowledge;

(8)   Duties assigned to the Headquarters under the provisions of laws and regulations, except as provided for in (1) to (7) above.

(Organization)

Article V

1.   The head of the Headquarters shall be the Chief of the International Peace Cooperation Headquarters (hereinafter referred to as ''the Chief'') and the Prime Minister shall be designated thereto.

2.   The Chief shall supervise the Headquarters in the conduct of business, and direct and supervise the personnel of the Headquarters divisions.

3.   The Headquarters shall have the Deputy Chief of the International Peace Cooperation Headquarters (referred to as ''the Deputy Chief'' in Paragraph 4 below) and the Chief Cabinet Secretary shall be designated thereto.

4.   The Deputy Chief shall assist the Chief in discharging the latter's responsibilities.

5.   The Headquarters shall have the members of the International Peace Cooperation Headquarters (hereinafter referred to as ''the Headquarters Members'' in this Article).

6.   The Headquarters Members shall be appointed by the Prime Minister from among the Ministers of State and the Heads of Administrative Agencies Concerned who have been designated beforehand under the provisions of Article 9 of the Cabinet Law (Law No. 5 of 1947).

7.   The Headquarters Members may advise the Chief concerning the duties of the Headquarters.

8.   In accordance with the provisions of Cabinet Order, there may be established in the Headquarters, for a specified period under each Implementation Plan, the Corps as an organization engaging directly in the implementation of International Peace Cooperation Assignments and undertaking the duties mentioned in Paragraph 2 (3) of Article IV above in Overseas Areas.

9.   The Secretariat shall be established within the Headquarters in order to deal with the duties of the Headquarters except for those undertaken by the Corps.

10.   The Secretariat shall have an executive secretary and other staff.

11.   The executive secretary shall be responsible for the management of the Secretariat under the instructions of the Chief.

12.   Except as provided for in the foregoing paragraphs of the present Article, matters necessary for the organization of the Headquarters shall be provided for in Cabinet Order.

Chapter III: International Peace Cooperation Assignments

(Implementation Plans)

Article VI

1.   The Prime Minister shall seek a decision of the Cabinet meeting for the implementation of International Peace Cooperation Assignments and a draft Implementation Plan,

when the implementation of International Peace Cooperation Assignments by Japan is deemed appropriate and the following consent has been obtained:

(1)   With regard to International Peace Cooperation Assignments undertaken for United Nations Peace-Keeping Operations: consent by the Parties to Armed Conflicts and host countries for the implementation of such assignments;

(2)   With regard to International Peace Cooperation Assignments undertaken for Humanitarian International Relief Operations: consent by host countries for the implementation of such assignments.

2.   An Implementation Plan shall provide for the following:

(1)   Basic policy for the implementation of International Peace Cooperation Assignments concerned;

(2)   Establishment of the Corps and other matters concerning the implementation of International Peace Cooperation Assignments concerned as follows:

(a) types and contents of International Peace Cooperation Assignments to be implemented;

(b) receiving countries and a period for which International Peace Cooperation Assignments are to be implemented;

(c) size and composition of the Corps and its equipment;

(d) the following matters in a case where the undertaking of International Peace Cooperation Assignments concerned involves the use of vessels or aircraft of the Maritime Safety Agency:

  (i) types and contents of International Peace Cooperation Assignments involving the use of vessels or aircraft of the Maritime Safety Agency;

  (ii) size and composition of the personnel of the Maritime Safety Agency to undertake International Peace Cooperation Assignments and the equipment thereof.

(e) the following matters in a case where the units and organs of the Self-Defence Forces referred to in Article 8 of the Self-Defence Forces Law (Law No. 165 of 1954) (hereinafter referred to as ''SDF Units'') undertake International Peace Cooperation Assignments concerned:

  (i) types and contents of International Peace Cooperation Assignments to be undertaken by SDF Units;

  (ii) size and composition of SDF Units to undertake International Peace Cooperation Assignments and the equipment thereof.

(f) scope of transportation which may be entrusted to the Director-General of the Maritime Safety Agency or the Director-General of the Defence Agency under the provisions of Paragraph 1 of Article XX below;

(g) matters of significance concerning cooperation of Administrative Agencies Concerned;

(h) other matters of significance concerning the implementation of International Peace Cooperation Assignments concerned.

United Nations University Press
53-70, Jingumae 5-chome
Shibuya-ku, Tokyo 150-8925
Japan

Reader's Reply Card

Global Financial Turmoil and Reform
A United Nations Perspective
Supervising Editor: Barry Herman

UNUP-1032   ISBN 92-808-1032-4

The information on this card will help us to improve our publishing programme. Please complete the card and return it to the United Nations University Press.

Name

Address

Country

What are your areas of interest?

Development. . . . . □
Social Sciences. . . . . □
Natural Resources. . . . . . . □
Economics . . . . □
Food and Nutrition . . . . . . □
Energy. . . . . □
International Law . . . . □
Politics. . . . . □
Culture. . . . . □
Science and Technology. . . □
Other. . . . . □

How did you come to know about this book?

□ UNU Press Publications Catalogue
□ Advertisement in. . . . .
□ Distributor. . . . .
□ Bookstore. . . . .
□ Other. . . . .

□ I am interested in information about the UNU . . . .

□ Please add my name to the catalogue mailing list. . . . .

3. The Minister for Foreign Affairs may, when he deems that he implementation of International Peace Cooperation Assignments is appropriate, request the Prime Minister to seek the decision of the Cabinet meeting referred to in Paragraph 1 above.

4. The equipment mentioned in Paragraph 2 (2) above shall be stipulated in an Implementation Plan within the scope of what is necessary for the implementation of the provisions of the present Chapter in light of the spirit of the provisions of Paragraph 2 of Article II and the provisions of Article III (1) and (2), provided that the equipment for International Peace Cooperation Assignments implemented for United Nations Peace-Keeping Operations shall be determined within the limits deemed necessary by the Secretary-General.

5. International Peace Cooperation Assignments undertaken by means of vessels or aircraft of the Maritime Safety Agency shall be stipulated in an Implementation Plan from among the tasks mentioned in (g) to (p) of Article III (3) or the tasks assimilated thereto mentioned in (q) of Article III (3) as prescribed by Cabinet Order and deemed appropriate to be implemented by means of vessels or aircraft of the Agency in light of the spirit of Article 25 of the Maritime Safety Agency Law (Law No. 28 of 1948), provided that such stipulation shall not hinder the performance of mission by the Agency.

6. International Peace Cooperation Assignments undertaken by SDF Units shall be stipulated in an Implementation Plan from among the tasks mentioned in (a) to (f) and (j) to (p) of Article III (3) or the tasks assimilated thereto mentioned in (q) of Article III (3) as prescribed by Cabinet Order and deemed appropriate to be implemented by SDF Units, provided that such stipulation shall not hinder the performance of mission by the Self-Defence Forces.

7. With regard to International Peace Cooperation Assignments undertaken by SDF Units which are the tasks mentioned in (a) to (f) of Article III (3) and the tasks assimilated thereto mentioned in (q) of Article III (3) as prescribed by Cabinet Order, the Prime Minister shall obtain approval of the Diet for the implementation of such assignments prior to the commencement of dispatch of SDF Units to be engaged in such assignments to Overseas Areas, in light of the fivefold basic principles governing Japan's participation in United Nations peace-keeping forces, i.e., the spirit of the provisions of Article III (1), Paragraphs 1 (1) and 13 (1) of the present Article, Paragraph 1 (6) of Article VIII and Article XXIV, as well as the purpose of this Law. If the Diet is closed or the House of Representatives is dissolved, such approval shall be sought without delay in the first Diet session subsequent to the commencement of dispatch of SDF Units engaged in such assignments to Overseas Areas.

8. When the approval of the Diet is requested from the Prime Minister under the provisions of the first sentence of Paragraph 7 above, the first House to which the request is submitted shall endeavour to make decision within seven days after such request of the Prime Minister, time in recess excepted, and the other House shall likewise do so within seven days after receipt of a bill passed by the said first House, time in recess excepted.

9. The Government shall terminate without delay International Peace Cooperation Assignments mentioned in Paragraph 7 above, when the Diet resolves upon disapproval under the provisions of the second sentence of the said Paragraph.

10. With regard to International Peace Cooperation Assignments mentioned in Paragraph 7 above, in order to extend the implementation thereof beyond the day two years after the date of the approval of the Diet obtained in accordance with the provisions of the said Paragraph, the Prime Minister shall submit, within a period from thirty days before that day to that day, a request pertaining to the continuation of such assignments to the Diet for its approval. If the Diet is closed or the House of Representatives is dissolved, such approval shall be sought in the first Diet session convened thereafter.

11. The Government shall terminate without delay International Peace Cooperation Assignments mentioned in Paragraph 7 above, when the Diet resolves upon disapproval under the provisions of Paragraph 10 above.

12. The provisions of Paragraphs 10 and 11 shall apply *mutatis mutandis* with regard to cases where it is planned to further extend the implementation of International Peace Cooperation Assignments mentioned in Paragraph 7 above beyond the period of two years after the original extension of the implementation of such assignments with the approval of the Diet.

13. The provisions of Paragraph 1, those of (1) and (2) excepted, and Paragraph 3 above shall apply *mutatis mutandis* with regard to revisions of an Implementation Plan including revisions pertaining to the termination of dispatch of the personnel engaged in International Peace Cooperation Assignments to Overseas Areas, which shall be effected in the cases mentioned below. The terms "deemed appropriate and the following consent has been obtained:" in Paragraph 1 and " deemed appropriate" in Paragraph 3 shall then read "deemed necessary or appropriate".

(1) With regard to International Peace Cooperation Assignments undertaken for United Nations Peace-Keeping Operations: a case where the agreement or consent mentioned in Article III (1) above or the consent mentioned in Paragraph 1 (1) of the present Article is deemed to have ceased to exist, or where the impartiality of such operations to any of the Parties to Armed Conflicts is deemed to have ceased to exist;

(2) With regard to International Peace Cooperation Assignments undertaken for Humanitarian International Relief Operations: a case where the consent or agreement mentioned in Article III (2) above or the consent mentioned in Paragraph 1 (2) of the present Article is deemed to have ceased to exist.

(Report to the Diet)

Article VII

The Prime Minister shall report the following matters, as the case may be, to the Diet without delay:

(1) In case of a decision or revision of an Implementation Plan: the contents of such plan as decided or revised;

(2)   In case of the termination of International Peace Cooperation Assignments provided for in the Implementation Plan: the result of the implementation of such assignments;

(3)   In case of an alteration of the period, provided for in the Implementation Plan, for which International Peace Cooperation Assignments are undertaken: the progress of implementation of such assignments during the period prior to the alteration.

(Operating Procedures)

Article VIII

1.   To implement International Peace Cooperation Assignments in accordance with the Implementation Plan, the Chief shall prepare, and revise if necessary, Operating Procedures which shall provide for details concerning such matters as referred to in (1) to (5) below as well as for matters referred to in (6) and (7) below:

(1)   Areas where International Peace Cooperation Assignments concerned are to be undertaken and the period during which they are to be undertaken;

(2)   Types and contents of International Peace Cooperation Assignments concerned for each area and period mentioned in (1) above;

(3)   Means to implement International Peace Cooperation Assignments concerned for each area and period mentioned in (1) above, including matters relating to equipment to be used for such assignments;

(4)   Matters concerning the personnel to be engaged in International Peace Cooperation Assignments concerned for each area and period mentioned in (1) above;

(5)   Matters concerning the relationship with the relevant authorities and inhabitants in receiving countries;

(6)   Matters concerning the suspension of International Peace Cooperation Assignments which shall be effected by the personnel engaged in such assignments in cases referred to in Paragraph 13 of Article VI;

(7)   Other matters which the Chief deems necessary for the implementation of International Peace Cooperation Assignments concerned.

2.   With regard to International Peace Cooperation Assignments to be implemented as United Nations Peace-Keeping Operations, the preparation and revision of Operating Procedures shall be made so as to conform with commands of the Secretary-General or a person who exercises the powers of Secretary-General in receiving countries, unless otherwise deemed necessary by the Chief as regards the matters referred to in Paragraph 1 (6) above.

3.   If deemed necessary, the Chief may delegate part of his powers for the preparation or revision of Operating Procedures to the designated personnel of the Corps.

(Implementation of International Peace Cooperation Assignments and Others)

Article IX

1.   The Corps shall undertake International Peace Cooperation Assignments in accordance with an Implementation Plan and Operating Procedures.

2.   In light of the spirit of the provisions of Paragraph 1 of Article II, the personnel of the Corps shall, when engaged in the duties referred to in Paragraph 2 (3) of Article IV, endeavour actively to collect information and data deemed useful for the proper discharge of such duties, in a manner responsive to changes of circumstances in the places where International Peace Cooperation Assignments are undertaken.

3.   At the request of the Chief for International Peace Cooperation Assignments referred to in Paragraph 5 of Article VI as set forth in the Implementation Plan, the Director-General of the Maritime Safety Agency may, in accordance with the Implementation Plan and Operating Procedures, direct its personnel who are the crew of the Agency's vessels or aircraft to undertake such assignments by means of such vessels or aircraft.

4.   At the request of the Chief for International Peace Cooperation Assignments referred to in Paragraph 6 of Article VI as set forth in the Implementation Plan, the Director-General of the Defence Agency may, in accordance with the Implementation Plan and Operating Procedures, direct SDF Units to undertake such assignments.

5.   When International Peace Cooperation Assignments are implemented under the provisions of Paragraphs 3 and 4 above, the personnel of the Maritime Safety Agency mentioned in Paragraph 3 or the personnel of the Self-Defence Forces in terms of paragraph 5 of Article 2 of the Self-Defence Forces Law (hereinafter referred to as "the SDF Personnel") who belong to SDF Units mentioned in Paragraph 4 above shall be engaged respectively in International Peace Cooperation Assignments concerned in accordance with the Implementation Plan and Operating Procedures.

6.   The Prime Minister shall determine matters concerning the relationship between the Chief and the Director-General of the Defence Agency in case of the undertaking of International Peace Cooperation Assignments by SDF Units under the provisions of Paragraph 4 above, except as provided for in this Law.

7.   The Corps shall maintain a close contact with such diplomatic establishments abroad as designated by the Minister for Foreign Affairs.

8.   The heads of diplomatic establishments abroad as designated by the Minister for Foreign Affairs shall, under the instruction of the Minister, extend cooperation necessary for the implementation of International Peace Cooperation Assignments.

(Appointment and Dismissal of the Personnel of the Corps)

Article X

The Chief shall appoint and dismiss the personnel of the Corps (hereinafter referred to as "the Corps Personnel")

(Employment of the Corps Personnel)

Article XI

1.   To engage them in International Peace Cooperation Assignments pertaining to the tasks mentioned in (g) to (p) of Article III (3) or the tasks assimilated thereto mentioned in

(q) of Article III (3) as prescribed by Cabinet Order, the Chief may employ by nomination the Corps Personnel with a specified term of mission from among such persons as volunteering to undertake such assignments.

2.   In dealing with the employment under the provisions of Paragraph 1 above, the Chief shall endeavour to seek cooperation from Administrative Agencies Concerned, local public authorities or private entities so as to ensure the extensive mobilization of talent.

(Assignment of the Personnel of Administrative Agencies Concerned to the Corps)
Article XII

1.   The Chief may, in accordance with the Implementation Plan, request the heads of Administrative Agencies Concerned to assign to the Corps such personnel, those referred to in (1) to (15), (17) and (18) of paragraph 3 of Article 2 of the National Civil Servant Law (Law No. 120 of 1947) excepted, as possessing skills, capabilities and other qualifications necessary for the implementation of International Peace Cooperation Assignments by the Corps, provided that the Prime Minister shall not request the personnel other than the SDF Personnel to be assigned to International Peace Cooperation Assignments pertaining to the tasks mentioned in (a) to (f) of Article III (3) and the tasks assimilated thereto mentioned in (g) of Article III (3) as prescribed by Cabinet Order.

2.   At the request under the provisions of Paragraph 1 above, the heads of Administrative Agencies Concerned shall, to the extent not to hinder the performance of the respective duties, assign to the Corps with a specified term of mission the personnel as described in the said Paragraph.

3.   The personnel assigned under the provisions of Paragraph 2 above, except for the SDF Personnel, shall be employed as the Corps Personnel with the term of mission referred to in the said Paragraph while maintaining their original government posts.

4.   The SDF Personnel assigned under the provisions of Paragraph 2 above shall be employed as the Corps Personnel with the term of mission referred to in the said Paragraph while being in possession both of the status of the Corps Personnel and that of the SDF Personnel.

5.   The personnel employed as the Corps Personnel either maintaining their original government posts according to the provisions of Paragraph 3 above or in possession both of the status of the Corps Personnel and that of the SDF Personnel according to the provisions of Paragraph 4 above shall be engaged in International Peace Cooperation Assignments under the direction and supervision of the Chief.

6.   With regard to the Corps Personnel assigned by the Director-General of the Defence Agency under the provisions of Paragraph 2 above (hereinafter referred to as ''the Corps Personnel from SDF'' in the present Article), the Prime Minister shall deprive such personnel of their status of the Corps Personnel in cases where the need of such assignment has ceased to exist and as otherwise provided for in Cabinet Order. Such SDF Personnel shall revert to the Self-Defence Forces.

7.   The Corps Personnel from SDF shall be deprived of their status of the Corps Personnel, if and when they are deprived of their status of the SDF Personnel.

8.   For the purposes of the laws and regulations concerning wages and other matters, i.e., wages other than the International Peace Cooperation Allowance stipulated in Article XVI, accident compensation and retirement allowance as well as cooperative society systems, the personnel in possession both of the status of the Corps Personnel and that of the SDF Personnel according to the provisions of Paragraph 4 above shall be regarded as belonging only to the Self-Defence Forces.

9.   Matters not included in Paragraphs 4 to 8 above which are necessary for treating the status of such personnel referred to in Paragraph 8 above shall be prescribed by Cabinet Order.

Article XIII

1.   When the Director-General of the Maritime Safety Agency directs its personnel to undertake International Peace Cooperation Assignments under the provisions of Paragraph 3 of Article IX above, the Director-General shall assign such personnel to the Corps for a specified period. Such personnel of the Agency thus assigned shall be employed as the Corps Personnel while maintaining their original government posts for the said period as the term of mission, and be engaged as the Corps Personnel in the duties referred to in Paragraph 2 (3) of Article IV above.

2.   When the Director-General of the Defence Agency directs SDF Units to undertake International Peace Cooperation Assignments under the provisions of Paragraph 4 of Article IX above, the Director-General shall assign the SDF Personnel belonging to SDF Units concerned to the Corps for a specified period. Such SDF Personnel thus assigned shall be employed as the Corps Personnel for the said period as the term of mission, possess both the status of the SDF Personnel and that of the Corps Personnel, and be engaged as the Corps Personnel in the duties referred to in Paragraph 2 (3) of Article IV above.

3.   Besides those contained in Paragraph 2 above, the provisions of Paragraphs 6 to 9 of Article XII above shall apply *mutatis mutandis* with regard to the treatment of the status of such personnel in possession both of the status of the SDF Personnel and that of the Corps Personnel according to the provisions of Paragraph 2 above.

(Exclusion of Application of the National Civil Servant Law)

Article XIV

With regard to the Corps Personnel employed according to the provisions of Paragraph 1 of Article XI above, the provisions of paragraph 1 of Article 103 as well as Article 104 of the National Civil Servant Law shall not apply, even though such personnel have assumed posts of executives, advisers or councillors (hereinafter jointly referred to as "Executives") in entities for the purposes of managing profit-making enterprises referred to in paragraph 1 of Article 103 of the said Law (hereinafter referred to as "Enterprises" in this Article) or managed the personnel's own Enterprises, or, with a reward, assumed posts of Executives, been engaged in undertakings or otherwise performed duties in entities for the purposes of undertakings other than Enterprises, before such personnel become the Corps personnel.

(Training)

Article XV

The Corps Personnel shall undergo training as designated by the Chief for the proper and effective implementation of International Peace Cooperation Assignments.

(International Peace Cooperation Allowance)

Article XVI

1.   International Peace Cooperation Allowance may be paid to the personnel engaged in International Peace Cooperation Assignments in view of the working conditions in receiving countries where such assignments are undertaken and of the characters of such assignments.

2.   Matters necessary for International Peace Cooperation Allowance referred to in Paragraph 1 above shall be prescribed by Cabinet Order.

3.   The Prime Minister shall ask the advice of the National Personnel Authority upon the enactment, amendment or abolishment of Cabinet Order mentioned in Paragraph 2 above.

(Uniforms)

Article XVII

1.   Uniforms of the Corps Personnel shall be set forth by Cabinet Order.

2.   Clothing may, in accordance with the provisions of Cabinet Order, be supplied or lent to the Corps Personnel that are necessary for performing their duties.

(Upper Limit of Total Number of Personnel Engaged in International Peace Cooperation Assignments)

Article XVIII

The total number of the personnel engaged in International Peace Cooperation Assignments shall not exceed two thousand.

(Regular Number of the Corps Personnel)

Article XIX

The regular number of the Corps Personnel shall be fixed by Cabinet Order for each of the Corps as may be necessary for the implementation of International Peace Cooperation Assignments in accordance with an Implementation Plan.

(Entrustment of Transportation)

Article XX

1. The Chief may, under an Implementation Plan, entrust to the Director-General of the Maritime Safety Agency or the Director-General of the Defence Agency the transportation of Affected People by vessels or aircraft to implement International Peace Cooperation Assignments mentioned in (k) of Article III (3) or the transportation of goods by vessels or aircraft to implement International Peace Cooperation Assignments mentioned in (j) to (o) of Article III (3), except for such transportation of Affected People or goods between the points within a receiving country or between the two adjacent receiving countries.

2. The Director-General of the Maritime Safety Agency or the Director-General of the Defence Agency may, upon the entrustment according to the provisions of Paragraph 1 above, accept and undertake the entrusted transportation to the extent not to hinder the performance of missions respectively by the Maritime Safety Agency or the Self-Defence Forces.

(Cooperation by Administrative Agencies Concerned)

Article XXI

1. If deemed necessary for the implementation of International Peace Cooperation Assignments by the Corps, the Chief may request the heads of Administrative Agencies Concerned for cooperation such as the transfer of ownership of goods under their respective jurisdictions.

2. The heads of Administrative Agencies Concerned shall, at the request according to the provisions of Paragraph 1 above, make such cooperation mentioned in the said Paragraph to the extent not to hinder the performance of the respective duties.

(Possession and Lending of Small-Sized Weapons)

Article XXII

The Headquarters may possess such types of small-sized weapons as prescribed by Cabinet Order which are necessary for securing the safety of the Corps Personnel.

Article XXIII

1. In engaging the Corps Personnel in International Peace Cooperation Assignments which the Corps undertakes in receiving countries under the provisions of Paragraph 1 of Article IX above, the Chief may lend to the Corps Personnel, during his stay in receiving countries, small-sized weapons mentioned in Article XXII above that shall be stipulated as equipment in the Implementation Plan according to the provisions of Paragraphs 2 (2) (c) and 4 of Article VI above, if deemed particularly necessary in view of the local safety conditions and other related factors.

2. The personnel of the Headquarters designated by the Chief for assuming the responsibility of controlling small-sized weapons may keep into custody such small-sized weapons as to lend to the Corps Personnel according to the provisions of Paragraph 1 above.

3.   Necessary matters relating to criteria for lending, control and other aspects of small-sized weapons shall be prescribed by Cabinet Order.

(Use of Arms)

Article XXIV

1.   The Corps Personnel engaged in International Peace Cooperation Assignments in receiving countries to whom small-sized weapons have been lent under the provisions of Paragraph 1 of Article XXIII above may use such small-sized weapons within the limits considered reasonably necessary under the circumstances concerned, if deemed that the unavoidable needs exist on a reasonable ground so as to protect life or person of their own or other Corps Personnel present with them on the same spot.

2.   The Maritime Safety Agency officers and sub-officers (hereinafter jointly referred to as "the MSA Officers" in this Article) engaged in International Peace Cooperation Assignments in receiving countries under the provisions of Paragraph 5 of Article IX above may use such small-sized weapons as carried by the MSA Officers concerned within the limits considered reasonably necessary under the circumstances concerned, if deemed that the unavoidable needs exist on a reasonable ground so as to protect life or person of their own or other personnel of the Maritime Safety Agency or Corps Personnel present with them on the same spot. The said small-sized weapons shall be such small-sized weapons as prescribed by Cabinet Order mentioned in Article XXIII above that shall be stipulated as equipment in the Implementation Plan according to the provisions of Paragraphs 2 (2) (d) (ii) and 4 of Article VI above.

3.   The members of the Self-Defence Forces engaged in International Peace Cooperation Assignments in receiving countries under the provisions of Paragraph 5 of Article IX above may use arms within the limits considered reasonably necessary under the circumstances concerned, if deemed that the unavoidable needs exist on a reasonable ground so as to protect life or person of their own or other SDF Personnel or Corps Personnel present with them on the same spot. The said arms shall be those stipulated as equipment in the Implementation Plan according to the provisions of Paragraph 2 (2) (e) (ii) and 4 of Article VI above.

4.   The use of small-sized weapons or arms under the provisions of the foregoing Paragraphs shall not cause harm to persons, except for cases corresponding to the provisions of Articles 36 and 37 of the Penal Code (Law No. 45 of 1907).

5.   The provisions of Article 20 of the Maritime Safety Agency Law shall not apply with regard to the MSA Officers engaged in International Peace Cooperation Assignments in receiving countries under the provisions of Paragraph 5 of Article IX above.

6.   The provisions of Article 95 of the Self-Defence Forces Law shall not apply with regard to the members of the Self-Defence Forces engaged in International Peace Cooperation Assignments in receiving countries under the provisions of Paragraph 5 of Article IX above.

7. With regard to the members of the Self-Defence Forces engaged in International Peace Cooperation Assignments in receiving countries under the provisions of Paragraph 5 of Article IX above, the provisions of paragraph 3 of Article 96 of the Self-Defence Forces Law shall not apply to offences committed by persons other than the SDF Personnel.

8. In case of the suspension of International Peace Cooperation Assignments mentioned in Paragraph 1 (6) of Article VIII above (hereinafter referred to as "Suspension" in this Paragraph), the provisions of Paragraph 1 above shall apply *mutatis mutandis* to the Corps Personnel involved in such assignments; likewise in case of Suspension, the provisions of Paragraphs 2 and 5 above shall apply *mutatis mutandis* to the MSA Officers involved in such assignments, the provisions of Paragraphs 3, 6 and 7 above to the members of the Self-Defence Forces thus involved. The provisions of Paragraph 4 above shall apply *mutatis mutandis* with regard to the use of small-sized weapons or arms according to the provisions of Paragraphs 1 to 3 above as herewith applied *mutatis mutandis*.

Chapter IV: Cooperation in Kind

(Cooperation in Kind)
Article XXV

1. The Government may extend Cooperation in Kind, if the Government deems it appropriate to extend such cooperation in order to cooperate for United Nations Peace-Keeping Operations or Humanitarian International Relief Operations.

2. The Prime Minister shall seek a decision of the Cabinet meeting for Cooperation in Kind.

3. The Minister for Foreign Affairs may request the Prime Minister to seek a decision of the Cabinet meeting concerning Cooperation in Kind, if he deems it appropriate to extend such cooperation in order to cooperate for United Nations Peace-Keeping Operations or Humanitarian International Relief Operations.

4. If deemed necessary for Cooperation in Kind, the Chief may request the heads of Administrative Agencies Concerned for the transfer of ownership of goods under their respective jurisdictions.

5. The heads of Administrative Agencies Concerned shall, at the request according to the provisions of Paragraph 4 above, transfer ownership of goods under their respective jurisdictions to the extent not to hinder the performance of the respective duties.

Chapter V: Miscellaneous Provisions

(Cooperation of Private Persons and Other Matters)
Article XXVI

1. If deemed impossible to implement fully International Peace Cooperation Assignments by arrangements under the provisions of Chapter III above or if deemed necessary

for purposes of Cooperation in Kind, the Chief may, with cooperation of the heads of Administrative Agencies Concerned, request those other than the State to cooperate for the alienation or loan of goods or the supply of service.

2.   The Government shall make payment of the proper cost to those other than the State thus requested for cooperation under the provisions of Paragraph 1 above, and shall make necessary financial arrangement for a loss incurred upon them caused by such cooperation.

(Delegation to Cabinet Order)

Article XXVII

Unless specifically provided in this Law, procedures for the execution of this Law and other matters necessary for its enforcement shall be prescribed by Cabinet Order.

Additional Provisions (Excerpt)

(Date of Entry into Force)

Article I

This Law shall come into force on the date to be set forth by Cabinet Order not later than three months from the date of its promulgation.

(Special Provisions Concerning International Peace Cooperation Assignments Undertaken by SDF Units)

Article II

International Peace Cooperation Assignments undertaken by SDF Units, which are the tasks mentioned in (a) to (f) of Article III (3) and the tasks assimilated thereto mentioned in (q) of Article III (3) as prescribed by Cabinet Order, shall not be implemented until the date to be set forth by a separate law.

(Review)

Article III

Upon the passage of three years after the entry into force of this Law the Government shall make a review concerning the arrangement for the execution of this Law in light of the state of the execution of this Law.

(Article IV to Article IX, which provide for necessary technical amendments of the relevant provisions of existing laws, are omitted)

Appendix regarding Article III

(1)   United Nations

(2)   Organs established by the General Assembly of the United Nations or the Specialized Agencies of the United Nations, as listed as follows or otherwise prescribed by Cabinet Order:

(a) Office of the United Nations Disaster Relief Coordinator (UNDRO)

(b) Office of the United Nations High Commissioner for Refugees (UNHCR)

(c) United Nations Relief and Works Agency for Palestine Refugees in the Near East (UNRWA)

(d) United Nations Children's Fund (UNICEF)

(e) United Nations Volunteers (UNV)

(f) United Nations Development Programme (UNDP)

(g) United Nations Environment Programme (UNEP)

(h) UN/FAO World Food Programme (WFP)

(i) Food and Agriculture Organization of the United Nations (FAO)

(j) World Health Organization (WHO)

(3) International Organization for Migration (IOM)

A detailed comment on the Law appears in pp. 33–73.

Source: *Japanese Annual of International Law*, no. 36, 1993, pp. 272–289.

Annex III

LAW CONCERNING DISPATCH OF JAPAN DISASTER RELIEF TEAMS, 1987

[September 16, 1987
Law number 93]
Entered into force on September 16, 1987
Amended by Law number 80 of June 19, 1992

(Purpose)

Article 1

The purpose of this Law is to provide for necessary measures relating to the dispatch of Japan Disaster Relief Teams consisting of personnel who will engage in international disaster relief activities in the event of large-scale disasters occurring or which threaten to occur overseas, especially in developing areas, in response to a request from the Government of a country stricken by a disaster or a country likely to suffer from such a disaster, or from an international organization (hereunder refer to as ''the Government of a disaster-stricken country etc.''), and thus to contribute to the promotion of international cooperation.

(Activities of Japan Disaster Relief Teams)

Article 2

A Japan Disaster Relief Team shall engage in the following disaster-related activities (hereunder refer to as ''international disaster relief activities'') as provided for in the preceding Article:

(1) search and rescue activities;

(2) medical care activities (including epidemic-prevention activities);

(3) activities to mitigate damage from the effects of a disaster, rehabilitation activities.

(Consultation with administrative organs concerned)

Article 3

1.   Upon receiving a request for the dispatch of a Japan Disaster Relief Team from the Government of a disaster-stricken country etc., the Minister for Foreign Affairs, when he deems it appropriate to dispatch a Team in the light of the purpose stated in Article 1, shall, for the purpose of obtaining their cooperation in order to facilitate the dispatch of a Japan Disaster Relief Team, consult with appropriate heads of the administrative organs listed in the Schedule (refer to as "an administrative organ concerned") or the National Public Safety Commission, when doing so, bearing in mind the nature of the request from the Government of the disaster-stricken country and the type and character of the disaster.

2.   Following consultation as provided for in the preceding Paragraph, the Minister for Foreign Affairs, when he deems it particularly necessary in the light of the purpose stated in Article 1, shall, for the purpose of obtaining its cooperation in order to facilitate activities as mentioned hereunder by its unit and other organ as provided for in Article 8 of Self Defence Force Law (Law number 165 of 1954), consult with the Director-General of the Defence Agency concerning:

(1)   International disaster relief activities;

(2)   Transportation of personnel who shall engage in international disaster relief activities or equipment and other materials necessary for those activities to areas overseas.

3.   The provisions of the preceding Paragraph, shall apply mutatis mutandis to the said activities, as provided for in Sub-Paragraph of the same Paragraph, by using a ship or aircraft of the Maritime Safety Agency. In such a case, the words "activities as mentioned hereunder by its unit and other organ as provided for in Article 8 of Self Defence Force Law (Law number 165 of 1954)" in that Paragraph shall read instead, "activities by using a ship or aircraft of the Maritime Safety Agency, as mentioned in Sub-paragraph 2" and "the Director-General of the Defence Agency" shall read instead, "the Director-General of the Maritime Safety Agency".

(Measures to be taken by the administrative organs concerned)

Article 4

The head of an administrative organ concerned may, on the basis of the consultation as provided for in Paragraph 1 of the preceding Article (in the case of the Director-General of the Maritime Safety Agency, Paragraph 2 of the same Article applied mutatis mutandis in Paragraph 1 or 3 of the same Article), order its personnel to engage in international disaster relief activities (in the case of personnel of the Maritime Safety Agency, the said activities shall include those as provided for in Paragraph 2 of the same Article, to be read instead by Paragraph 3 of the same Article).

2.   The Director-General of the Defence Agency may, on the basis of the consultation as provided in Paragraph 2 of the preceding Article, order its unit or other organ to engage in the activities as mentioned in each Sub-Paragraph of the same Paragraph.

3. The National Public Safety Commission may, on the basis of the consultation as provided for in Paragraph 1 of the preceding Article, instruct appropriate prefectural police forces to order their personnel to engage in international disaster relief activities.

4. A prefectural police force, when so instructed, may order its personnel to engage in international disaster relief activities.

5. The Director-General of the Fire-Defence Agency may, on the basis of the consultation as provided for in Paragraph 1 of the preceding Article, request appropriate municipal governments of a city, town or village to order personnel of their fire-defence organs to engage in international disaster relief activities.

6. The municipal government of a city, town or village, when so requested, may order personnel of its fire-defence organ to engage in international disaster relief activities.

(Order of the Minister for Foreign Affairs to the Japan International Cooperation Agency)

Article 5

1. The Minister for Foreign Affairs, when he deems it appropriate to do so in order to achieve the purpose stated in Article 1, may order the Japan International Cooperation Agency to dispatch national government or local public entity personnel who will engage in international disaster relief activities as provided for in the preceding Article, or personnel of the said Agency or other personnel as members of a Japan Disaster Relief Team.

2. Following consultation as provided for in Paragraph 1 or 2 of Article 3 (including cases where mutatis mutandis shall apply in Paragraph 3 of the same Article) the order provided for in the preceding Paragraph shall be given in accordance with the result of that consultation.

(Activities of Japan Disaster Relief Teams)

Article 6

1. The Minister for Foreign Affairs shall maintain close contact with the Government of the disaster-stricken country and coordinate the activities of the Japan Disaster Relief Team, taking into consideration the requests of the Government of the disaster-stricken country and other relevant factors.

2. A Japan Disaster Relief Team shall carry out its activities giving all due consideration to the requests of the Government of the disaster-stricken country.

(Activities of the Japan International Cooperation Agency)

Article 7

The dispatch of a Japan Disaster Relief Team and other tasks necessary for such dispatch (including the procurement of equipment and other materials necessary for the activities of the Japan Disaster Relief Team and the making of arrangements for the transportation of such equipment and materials, but excluding those tasks related to activities that come under Sub-Paragraph 2 of Paragraph 2 of Article 3 out of those as provided for in the same paragraph (including cases where mutatis mutandis shall apply in

Paragraph 3 of the same Article)) shall be carried out by the Japan International Cooperation Agency.

Supplementary Provisions

(Date of entry into force)
    Article 1.   This law shall enter into force as from the date of its promulgation.

Schedule
(relating to Article 3)
National Police Agency
Defence Agency
Science and Technology Agency
Environment Agency
National Land Agency
Ministry of Education
Ministry of Health and Welfare
Ministry of Agriculture, Forestry and Fisheries
Ministry of International Trade and Industry
Agency of Natural Resources and Energy
Ministry of Transport
Maritime Safety Agency
Meteorological Agency
Ministry of Posts and Telecommunications
Ministry of Labor
Ministry of Construction
Fire-Defence Agency

Source: Unofficial translation provided by the Ministry of Foreign Affairs, Economic Cooperation Bureau, Office of International Emergency Relief, 31 October 1995.

SELECT BIBLIOGRAPHY

In English

George, Aurelia. 1993. "Japan's participation in UN peacekeeping operations: Radical departure or predictable response?" *Asian Survey*, vol. 33, no. 6 (June), pp. 560–575.

Harrison, Selig S. and Masashi Nishara, eds. 1995. *UN Peacekeeping: Japanese and American Perspectives*. New York: Carnegie Endowment.

Heinrich, L. William Jr. 1997. "Seeking an honored place: The Japanese Self Defense Forces and the use of armed force abroad." Ph.D. dissertation, Columbia University.

Ogata, Sadako. 1990. "The United Nations and Japanese diplomacy." *Japan Review of International Affairs,* Fall/Winter, pp. 141–165.

Shibata, Akiho. 1994. "Japanese peace-keeping legislation and recent developments in U.N. operations." *Yale Journal of International Law*, vol. 19, no. 2 (Summer) pp. 307–348.

Yanai, Shunji. 1993. "Law Concerning Cooperation for United Nations Peace-keeping Operations and Other Operations." *Japanese Annual of International Law*, no. 36, pp. 33–73.

In Japanese

Kozai, Shigeru. 1991. *Kokuren no Heiwa Iji Katsudo* [UN peace-keeping operations]. Tokyo: Yuhikaku.

Sasaki, Yoshitaka. 1992. *Umi wo Wataru Jieitai: PKO Rippo to Seiji Kenryoku* [The Self-

Defence Forces cross the sea: The PKO legislation and political power]. Tokyo: Iwanami Shoten.

Shinyo, Takahiro. 1995. *Kokusai Heiwa Kyoryoku Nyumon* [An introduction to international peace cooperation]. Tokyo: Yuhikaku.

Takai, Susumu. 1995. *Kokuren PKO to Heiwa Kyoryokuho* [UN peace-keeping and the law]. Tokyo: Shinseisho.

INDEX